Creating an Authentic Youth Ministry

Edward M. Fashbaugh, II

DISCIPLESHIP RESOURCES

PO BOX 340003 • NASHVILLE, TN 37203-0003

www.discipleshipresources.org

To my wife Amy, who kept urging me to write;
to our children Zach and Gabi, who fill my life with joy;
and to Phillip and Matthew, who have been
great companions in Christ.

Cover and book design by Joey McNair

ISBN 0-88177-406-5

Library of Congress Control Number 2003102095

DR406

Contents

No Quick Fix

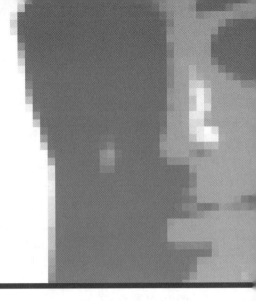

E very church that calls me wants to reach more youth. Every
church I go to wants to reach more youth. The desire to reach
more youth is embedded in our churches, and there is a real sense
that if we fail to reach teens, our particular church will have a difficult
time surviving. With all this desire to reach youth, why are mainline
churches overwhelmingly failing to reach a new generation of teens?
This book will examine that question and provide solutions that may
take your church from simply *a desire to reach youth* to *actually reaching today's teens* so that they become your partners in ministry.

A Principle-Centered Approach to Authentic Youth Ministry

Within the pages of this book, I intend to move beyond a static
understanding of youth ministry, through the mystery of it, and to an
approach that will bring lasting results in your church. As you read, I
hope you will be encouraged to think about the state of your youth ministry, motivated to ask questions, and inspired to test ideas.

Throughout the book, I will describe a principle-centered approach to
youth ministry. This approach will affect your church's ability to create a
foundation from which your youth ministry will flourish.

I have written this book in a conversational tone, as if you and I were
sitting down to talk. I want to be clear that this is not written to be a theological presentation on youth ministry, but instead comes from seven
years of observing and reflecting on the ministries I have encountered in

hundreds of churches. My hope is that this book will be a practical guide to help you revitalize not only your youth ministry, but also your church's entire ministry to all people.

If there has been a constant in my life, it has been my struggle with weight control since I was a teen. Oh, I could lay blame if I wanted to. I could blame our culture and the constant barrage of commercials that highlights the virtues of fast food fulfilling every hunger at any hour of the night. I could blame church events, such as ice cream socials, bake sales, cookie walks, pancake breakfasts, autumn corn roasts, pizza parties, potluck suppers, spaghetti dinners, Halloween hayrides with donuts and apple cider, Christmas Eve buffet lines, and, let's not forget, Easter morning's hot-crossed buns! If you have been around churches for any length of time, you know the mega-opportunities there are for eating all kinds of food and adding all kinds of weight. Is it any wonder that we do not find many Overeaters Anonymous groups in our churches? They would never make it! It would be like holding an AA meeting at an open bar!

In my life's struggle with weight, I have resorted to just about every fad diet ever known. I have done the starvation diet, the milkshake diet, the diet-pill diet, the low-carb diet, the liquid food-processing diet, and the Twinkie Diet. (Don't ask.) Believe it or not, I have lost a good amount of weight over the years. In fact, I calculated it once and discovered that I had lost at least a total equal to my entire body weight— twice! Here is the dilemma: even though I lost all that weight, I eventually discovered ways to find it again. Like a yo-yo, my weight would go down and back up, down and back up.

Finally, with my wife's loving instruction, I came to realize that weight loss and weight control are possible, but they take discipline, commitment, and the ability to see that the most effective weight-loss or weight-control routine is based on a well portioned, balanced diet, along with appropriate levels of fitness training. For most of us, true weight control is not found in a diet plan that circumvents good nutrition and exercise. Simple, isn't it? Lower the caloric input, and increase the caloric output. So why don't more people follow that simple plan? Because it is not easy; it takes discipline.

OK, I know you are thinking, "What in the world does this have to do with youth ministry?" Well, here's the point that I want to make right from the start: You picked up this book because it peaked your interest.

You are concerned about your youth ministry. Perhaps you have read a dozen books before and, like my weight, your youth ministry is having a yo-yo reaction. You make some great gains, only to be followed by set-backs. Or you look back over the youth ministry in your church, and you and others are able to recall a time when the church experienced a vital youth ministry, but there was never a way to sustain it.

Just as gimmick diets are used for quick weight loss, churches use special youth programs, activities, and outings to boost numbers that are rarely sustained. Just as gimmick diets rarely sustain true weight loss, gimmick ideas and creative activities rarely sustain an active ministry to and with teens.

Plenty of books and programs on the market promise you instant success if you try them. These fad plans will tell you, "If you just do what we did, if you follow these steps, if you put into action our keys for success, you too will have a vital program." Although some gifted youth ministry teams may be able to recreate other churches' successes, many more will feel discouraged and burned out when they simply cannot duplicate what took place in another church, even if they have followed all the prescribed steps.

So, straight up: if you are looking for a quick fix for your youth ministry woes, this book will not help. You have my permission to return it, get your money back, and purchase a book that offers bright new ideas and cool gimmicks to attract more teens to "instant" youth programs for fifty-two Sundays.

If, however, you are tired of trying the newest youth ministry model that worked at some other church; if you are tired of gimmicks; if your charismatic appeal is less than superstar status; and if you are ready to be disciplined and committed to a strategy that will bring lasting results, then this book will help you uncover the principles needed to develop the youth ministry your church truly desires. This book will help you discover a principle-centered approach to youth ministry that will impact teens for a lifetime and give your church a foundation that will not shift with each new wave of teens or with each new youth director. Only when your church is actively working to implement these principles will it have the foundation on which a long-term, high-impact youth ministry becomes reality. Only when these principles are activated will you discover a youth ministry that is no longer personality-driven, but principle-driven.

My Personal Quest

Looks like you're sticking it out with me, so let's get serious about committing to a new understanding of your church's ministry to and with youth. As we get ready for this journey, perhaps you should know a little more about me beyond my weight-loss struggle.

I recently became the lead pastor of a congregation. For the past seven years, though, I worked for the East Ohio Conference of The United Methodist Church as an associate conference council director for youth ministry. Before entering this judicatory ministry, I was a pastor in one church, youth pastor in two additional churches, the former East Ohio Conference of The United Methodist Church senior high youth coordinator, and, while in college, I served with a Young Life team. Additionally, I spent two summers on a camp staff for the Salvation Army and one summer on a YMCA day camp staff for inner-city children and youth. In all, I bring nearly twenty years of diverse experience to the material you will find in these pages.

In East Ohio, I served a denominational area of The United Methodist Church that consisted of 820 congregations covering just about every cultural context imaginable. My basic responsibilities were to assist our Conference Council on Youth Ministry in developing events for local congregations, to provide training for adults in youth ministry, and to give guidance and resource support to local churches. It was in my role as consultant that I had the privilege of visiting many churches located in a variety of cultural contexts.

OK, now that you have the scoop on me, can we be real here for a moment? When I first took the conference job, I thought I knew the answers to youth ministry problems. I had my "tool kit" of all the "successful" models that were working in some churches. I had all kinds of program resources, and I was schooled on teen culture.

It was not long into my ministry that I began getting calls from churches asking for help with their youth ministries. All I thought I would have to do was simply tell them about some of the current successful models, provide some program ideas, and leave an action plan that would ignite their passion for youth ministry. I had a toolbox full of gimmicks. (I had not yet learned from my dieting experiences.)

Not long after entering this ministry, I discovered that my task would not be as easy as I had thought. I came to realize that I was peddling a quick-fix approach to youth ministry that was too often coming up empty. Admittedly, I had been arrogant enough to think that I knew what a church needed for youth ministry before I even met with the church leaders. Do not misunderstand me here—there was nothing wrong with what I was telling people; in fact, they got excited about the possibilities. But there was something missing; something was not connecting. It was not until about three years into the job that I began to notice what was missing as I continued to meet with churches and grow in my own understanding of the dynamics facing church ministry in general, and youth ministry in particular.

I discovered certain themes running through my consultations and training seminars. There were common questions emerging, regardless of the cultural context. These questions needed something more than simple answers and a quick-fix plan. In just about every church I visited, regardless of size or economic status, I continued to hear these basic questions:

- How do we bring more teenagers to the church?
- How do we keep them once they come?
- How do we get them to come back once they have left?
- How do we get volunteers to work with teenagers?
- What programs are working to get and keep teenagers?
- Why don't our teenagers attend the worship service?
- Should we hire someone to do youth ministry?
- Is it OK for parents to be youth advisors?

Have you ever asked any of these questions? Maybe one or two led you to pick up this book.

Because these questions were being asked in just about every church and context, I was beginning to see that simply providing models and programs would not provide adequate answers or solutions. More and more, I realized that all these questions were directing me toward something more than universal answers and quick-fix solutions. I began asking myself what was beneath all these questions. Why did so many of our mainline churches, regardless of the context, share similar issues related to youth ministry?

Digging deeper and moving beyond all the youth ministry seminars I had ever attended, I began to believe that there had to be universal principles that could be applied to these questions, regardless of the cultural context. As I looked for these principles, they started to emerge from a number of sources, including discussions with others, books, Internet research, and God's direction in prayer. The more questions I heard, the more questions I asked as I moved closer to realizing these principles. In most cases, the questions led right back to the local church.

I began to look at how people understood their purpose and mission. I tried to feel their passion and uncover their deeper motivation for having youth as more than just a future generation to help the church survive. My quest for understanding became the focus of this book. The questions provided the context around which the principle-centered approach was developed.

What You Will Find in This Book

As you read this book, each chapter will offer a particular principle to study, reflect on, and consider. I encourage you to read this book with a group of people so that you can be on the journey together, and as more people become awakened, the likelihood of transformation will become greater in your church.

At the end of each chapter, you will find a series of "Now What?" questions that will help you and your team reflect on the status of that particular principle in your church. Where your principles are already established, celebrate, but then move forward, and continue to find those principles that still need to be developed or that have gone dormant in your church.

To uncover the principles of a healthy youth ministry, Chapter One will look at **youth ministry as part of the entire church ministry.** We will see why churches have struggled with maintaining long-term youth ministries and discover the root causes of a youth ministry that just cannot sustain vitality.

In Chapter Two, we will look at Principle # 1: **A healthy youth ministry flows from an intentional ministry of faith formation to and with adults.** Once you begin to think about it, this really becomes basic common sense. If we are not reaching adults, helping them to find hope, compassion, forgiveness, and new life in Christ, how can we ever expect to have a lasting, high-impact youth ministry? We will look at how this principle is the foundation on which a healthy youth ministry is built.

Chapter Three focuses on Principle #2: **A healthy youth ministry understands the positive expression of teen empowerment.** This has got to be the most abused concept in mainline church youth ministry today. We have taken a powerful concept and boiled it down to making sure teens have a voice and a vote on church committees. We will look at this misconception and try to get to a functional, helpful understanding of a more positive expression of teen empowerment.

Chapter Four will focus on Principle #3: **A healthy youth ministry understands the difference between youth activity and youth ministry.** Not long after I began consulting with churches, I realized that they were not really asking me to help them develop youth ministries, but instead they wanted me to help them develop teen activity programs. We will look at the differences between what it means to have a youth ministry and what it means to have an activity-driven program for teens.

The discussion about youth ministry versus youth activity leads right into Chapter Five and our look at Principle #4: **A healthy youth ministry intentionally recruits a diverse team of spiritually open and spiritually developing adult leaders.** Youth ministry was never meant to be a one-to-twenty proposition between one youth leader and a group of teens. In this chapter, we will focus on establishing a youth ministry where adults take an active role. We will look at how the entire ministry will be enhanced and vitalized by having a diverse group of adults who share a common understanding of the mission and purpose of their ministry to and with youth.

Chapter Six discusses Principle #5: **A healthy youth ministry has an intentional process for teen spiritual formation.** In order to provide the passion, inspiration, and motivation needed to assist people in their spiritual journeys, the youth ministry needs to have an intentional approach, or method, to provide teens with a strategy for their personal spiritual development. Throughout this chapter, we will take an in-depth look at how the church can develop a spiritual-formation process that assists teens in moving deeper into their spiritual journeys with Christ.

Chapter Seven uncovers Principle #6: **A healthy youth ministry is in constant transformation.** When youth ministry is based on principles, rather than on a program idea or a gimmick, it is in a far better position to adjust and shift to the changing culture. What works with one generation of teens may not work with another. It is important that the youth ministry see itself as a living organism in a process of constant growth and development.

Finally, in Chapter Eight we will **review the principles and make our plan to launch an intentional process** of developing a ministry to and with teens.

As you read this book, my hope is that you will be challenged, encouraged, and inspired to build a youth ministry that:
- impacts teens today and for years to come;
- outlasts the current fads;
- stands, regardless of how long the youth pastor or volunteers stay;
- is an authentic expression of spiritual formation;
- grounds teens firmly as disciples of Jesus Christ.

Your church has a mission to reach teens, and in your community there are all kinds of teens to reach. Will you take the pathway that leads to a long-term impact, or will you take a quick-fix route? If you can be patient and trust, then you will find that a principle-centered approach will go the distance and bring the real changes you want. Discipline and commitment, two difficult attributes, will not only give you and your church the youth ministry you seek, but also the youth ministry you are called to have.

Before we begin, I want you to know my biases. I believe that the church exists to continue the redemptive work of Jesus Christ in this world. I believe that the church community becomes a mission outpost for Jesus Christ, as well as a center of spiritual formation for those who are intentionally seeking to deepen their spiritual journeys. I believe that the primary purpose of being in ministry to and with teens is to assist teens in discovering the power of Jesus Christ in their lives. When adults are able to connect with teens on this level, the lives of both teens and adults are enriched in ways they could never have imagined.

I believe that adults are needed to connect with teens. This connection is called many things:
- a spiritual friendship;
- a mentor relationship;
- a coaching relationship.

You will see that I often use the term *coach* to refer to the teen-adult relationship. I like the image of a coach, because teens today are used to having coaches, instructors, directors, leaders, and guides in their everyday lives. The church is an organism within the current cultural reality of student life, and so it is appropriate to use images of this culture to assist in the spiritual formation of teens.

I know that there are all kinds of interpretations for what coach and leader mean, but for my purposes, the following definition will be used: coaches are people who are able to teach, instruct, listen, guide, develop strategies, continue learning, and evaluate, because they have traveled and are traveling the spiritual journey themselves. Coaches do not try to teach where they have not been, and they certainly do not develop strategies for things that they do not know. A coach realizes that the player he or she is developing today will be a coach to someone else, either during the same practice or sometime in the future.

Remember, this book is not about quick fixes to any of the problems we will encounter. It does not offer Band-Aid approaches or simple steps to success. The principles uncovered here will provide some short-term results to your church's overall ministry, but even more, they will lay the groundwork for a youth ministry that will not go up and down like my weight did on fad diets. If this book is anything, it is a guide to developing foundational principles that will ensure the stability, vitality, and authenticity of a long-term, high-impact ministry to and with teenagers.

With all this understood, let's get on with it.

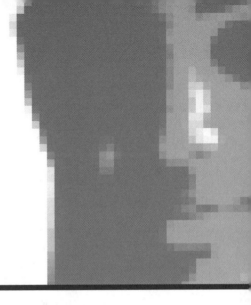

Chapter One
Sound Familiar?

"**W**hen *our* kids were teens, we had a strong youth ministry. Thirty years ago, we had youth group every Sunday! The Sunday school classes at all age levels were full. We remember how the youth went on retreats, did bake sales, helped with rummage sales, had a choir, came to worship (they sat in the back, but they were there), and every spring, they even planted flowers around the church. They were active and part of the church. Then the youth group leaders moved away, and, over the years, little by little, everything just seemed to fade away.

"We feel the teens today are missing out on this experience, and we want to help them regain it. We want them to have the kind of experiences our kids had. We need to do something, but nothing we do seems to make a difference. There are teens in the neighborhood, but we just cannot seem to bring them or their families into the church."

The Myth of "The Way It Was"

Sound familiar? Apart from the questions listed in the introduction, this is by far the most common scenario presented when I consult with churches. Usually some long-time member will recall the glory days of a "vital" youth group—when children filled the aisles during the worship service as they moved up to the children's moments. They remember teenagers helping with church activities and service projects. Without exception, the stories are always related to a particular pastor, youth minister, or parent(s) who led youth during those happy times.

Just about every church struggling with the vitality of its youth ministry remembers when it was different—when it was perceived to be a vital part of the overall church experience. So the solution to its current problem seems obvious: just help us get back to the way it was.

Over the years, church members have built up the glory days so much that their story often reaches mythical proportions. They believe this myth so deeply that they are always in search of getting it back to the way it was when everything was good. They go on their own version of the Search for the Holy Grail—if they could just find it.... But like the Grail, it is always just out of reach.

It is at these times that we need reality checks to help people see that the glory days may not have been all that glorious. But who wants to mess with people's illusions? Let's not dwell on it. The point here is that many mainline churches are not reaching youth *today*. They remember when they did reach youth—or at least when they had more youth in church. They struggle with the reality that they no longer see vital youth programs in their churches, and they want to do something about it.

The hard-core reality is that these stories, unfortunately, reveal more about the church than they do about the state of the church's youth ministry. In fact, these stories only reinforce the short-term vision most churches have had for youth ministry over the past several decades. The underlying theme is that as long as the youth are cared for by someone or some group of people in the church, the overall church can feel like it is doing what is expected of it for the next generation: provide a wholesome, fun, safe program that includes some religious training.

Youth Ministry and the Overall Life of the Church

The questions in the introduction and the stories above point to a fundamental misunderstanding of the role or place of youth ministry in the overall life of the church. In many churches, youth ministry is seen as something set apart from the overall church ministry. Youth Group has become an add-on—a necessary church program. Too often, youth ministry is seen as a responsibility, rather than a dynamic expression of the overall ministry of the church. Granted, the fact that churches are concerned about not having youth tells us that they take seriously the responsibility to reach each generation. The problem is that they just do not know how to effectively fulfill that responsibility. Hence, the temptation is to fall back on memories of when it was good.

Help me out here. Have you ever been in a worship service where the children's message simply served as a cute addition to the overall service? Sometimes the real point of the children's moment is simply to gather the children together so that they may leave for Junior Church, or even worse, the children's message is used to teach a vital truth with a simple story—to *adults*! Some pastors may even admit (if you ask) that the best aspect of the children's moment is that it provides the opportunity to present the central idea of the coming sermon in a way that is concise and understandable to everyone.

People like the children's message. I have been in churches where only one or two children come to the main worship service, and the adults *still* insist on having the children's sermon. For the children? No! The adults want it. Everyone likes the story or lesson, and they like to see the children, but there is really no point to the message *for the children*. It is just a nice add-on.

Well, that is exactly the attitude I frequently see toward youth ministry. They know they should do it, they believe in it, and they want to see it. Yet they do not know what to do with it when they have it. It is just a disconnected part of the overall ministry of the church.

Rarely did any mainline church I consult with ever see youth ministry as a strategic component of reaching the entire neighborhood for Christ. More and more, I encountered an attitude that considered youth ministry important, but little more than a program for the teens in the church. Seldom did any church articulate a vision for youth ministry that moved from a focus on *our* teens to *all* teens in the neighborhood. Youth outside the church were not even on the radar screen, but why should they be?

Most churches view their "ministries" as ministries for their own people, rather than part of a ministry to reach the world for Christ. This attitude, that youth ministry is somewhat disconnected from the rest of the church, began to help me see clearly why youth ministry was failing to become a vital element in most churches.

That said, I do not want to be too hard on these churches because they at least acknowledge the need to have something for *their* teens, and many have the sense that a strong youth program will be attractive to families with children and teens. This, at least, is a start.

Something else began to enter my frame of awareness that I had never seen before. In every church I consulted, I began to look at its overall ministry. These churches not only lacked vital youth ministries, but it could be argued that they had few, if any, vital ministries at all. Not only did youth not attend, but worship attendance among adults had dropped, as had adult Sunday school attendance. Church socials were not as well attended at they had once been, and worship was less than inspirational.

These two items—the disconnection between youth ministry and the overall ministry of the church, as well as the apparent connection between a youth vitality and adult vitality—finally made me look at youth ministry differently. I began to see that youth ministry is part of a whole that must be interconnected, rather than separated. It is this interconnection that has to be examined if a church is going to experience a long-term, meaningful youth ministry.

Up to this point, I too had taken a narrow approach to youth ministry by working just with the youth ministry team, assisting them with programs that would primarily affect only their group. I had to accept the reality that I myself had bought into the prevailing belief that youth ministry was something we *should do*, even if it really had no specific connection with the church's overall strategic plan. I really did think we could make a vital youth ministry happen in spite of the church's inability to have a vital ministry overall. I thought that perhaps, in some magical way, we could reach teens even if we could not reach adults. With gifted youth ministers, youth can be reached, but the results will always be temporary, unless youth ministry is part of the church's entire strategic plan to make *all* people disciples of Jesus Christ.

My experience in these churches began to challenge my belief system. As with the children's moments, if we were going to have vital youth ministries, then we must have ministry with purpose and connection to the whole, rather than just a nice add-on. Without these elements, our efforts were simply not going to produce long-term results. I was not going to be satisfied with simply providing nice ideas anymore. I saw that the church was in a crisis, and that crisis needed to be addressed if the church was ever going to have a long-term, meaningful, authentic youth ministry.

Little by little, I discovered that if a youth ministry was less than functional, it was not necessarily due to the youth pastor, the lack of parental involvement, or teen apathy. To be sure, these things can play a part, but they are really only surface issues. On a far deeper level, I was beginning to see that the ills noticeable in youth ministry were only symptomatic of the ills affecting the whole church. In other words, if a church was experiencing an anemic youth ministry, the source was deeper than the involvement of teens and parents, and deeper still than the issues surrounding the youth pastor (in most cases). Get this: *I have become convinced that if a church is experiencing an anemic youth ministry, the source is the overall spiritual anemia suffered within the total church community.* In both general and specific ways, our youth ministry reflects the strengths and weaknesses of the overall ministry of the church.

Vital Ministry with Youth

If mainline churches as a whole are finding it difficult to reach teens, are teens the issue? Or is the issue the overall spiritual life of the church? I contend, and will develop throughout this book, that the inability of a church to reach and keep teens is more about that church's spiritual condition than it is about the teen culture.

I first began to notice a vast difference in churches with vital youth ministries from those that were stagnating or struggling to survive. In the churches where youth ministry thrived, I witnessed one of two things:

(1) I saw churches where a dynamic youth pastor or volunteer was growing a youth group due to a charismatic personality. These churches had found their "ideal" youth minister in someone who was totally there for the teens. This youth minister made things both fun and spiritual, was able to be a friend to all kids, and seemed to be at all the kids' activities. In all these churches, the members were enthused and blessed because the youth ministry was almost instantly growing—they seemed to have found God's appointed servant.

OK, I'm going to say it, but before I do, I want you to remember what I said in the introduction. We are looking for foundational principles that will give us long-lasting, meaningful, and authentic results. Instant results in youth ministry often fade as quickly as fad-diet results. We are dealing with the good versus the best.

I am not even interested anymore when a church tells me about the great youth ministry that has developed since the new youth pastor came on board, especially when that great youth pastor is doing it all alone. I am not impressed because I know the probability of that new surge in youth ministry lasting beyond that new youth minister is minimal at best. If that gifted youth minister is not building a team and empowering adults to be in ministry to and with youth, then the probability diminishes even more. Even if the youth pastor *is* doing these things, when the overall church community is not intentionally on the journey, I know the chances of a long-term, authentic youth ministry will be minimal.

Maybe you are one of these gifted youth ministers who has come to a church and developed a growing youth ministry, and you wonder what in the world I am talking about. In fact, you may even be asking why you should read any further. Listen up, friend. Don't you back off on me now!

The results you have had are because you have gifts, relational skills, and something that is attractive to teens. The real test of a youth ministry, however, is not about how many teens attend, but about how much ownership the overall church has in the youth ministry.

What foundational principles are in place to sustain the ministry when you leave? Is it really the church's youth ministry, or is it your youth ministry? If they didn't have the ministry before you arrived, what do you think their chances of keeping it vital and authentic will be once you leave?

Should you give up on what you are doing? No way! But stay with me, and I will show you how to help that church build a foundation for a vital, authentic youth ministry that will last long after you have gone.

(2) The second thing I witnessed in churches developing authentic, vital youth ministries was a definite and holistic approach to building all people—children, youth, and adults—as disciples of Jesus Christ. The source of their overall vitality came from an authentic focus on ministry to and with adults. These churches had a strategic plan to reach all people for Jesus Christ. These churches put a high value on passionate spirituality and motivational worship experiences. These churches expected adults to enter into Bible studies, prayer groups, and other kinds of spiritual-formation opportunities.

It is rare to find a vital, long-term, high-impact, authentic youth ministry in a church absent of an intentionally discipling ministry to and with adults. It is rare to find a growing youth ministry in a church where membership is in decline. It is rare to find pumped-up teens for Christ in a church where adults are complacent about their own spiritual journeys. It is rare to experience vital youth ministries in a church where worship is not alive and full of passion. Maybe you can point to an exception, but again, the exception will likely be due to a dynamic, high-energy, passionate youth minister. These exceptions are simply that: exceptions, and not the norm.

We know that when the dynamic leader leaves (and they usually do eventually), the youth ministry will most likely cease to be the exception and will revert to the norm; that is, people wondering what has happened to their vital youth ministry. When this happens, and it will, the youth council director or the pastor will call me to come in for a consultation, and I will hear all over again about how their church once had a great youth ministry and how they want it back.

Once I became convinced that youth ministry was so intimately connected to the overall health of the church, I found myself unable to simply go and talk to a church about its youth ministry without looking at its overall ministry. I began to see how youth ministry, as all ministries, is interdependent with many factors in the life of the church: leadership, worship, discipleship, spiritual passion, and so forth. These factors are simply too critical to the overall effectiveness of youth ministry to ignore.

When we see this connection between youth ministry and the overall church ministry, we approach the place where we can build the foundation for an effective youth ministry. Please allow me to pound this concept into your consciousness: everything in the church fits together like a living organism. The health of one part of the organism is dependent on the overall well-being of the entire organism. Why are so many mainline churches struggling with a ministry to and with youth? The answer will only be found when we look at the real question: why are so many mainline churches struggling with vital ministries to and with adults?

If the overall ministry is not reviewed and studied in the context of how it relates to youth ministry, then the youth ministry is destined to repeat a yo-yo pattern. In this pattern, the youth ministry will only be as successful as the current youth leader is gifted, charismatic, and caring.

The majority of churches that I consult with already realize that not every church is blessed with a highly gifted, all-around great person to lead youth ministry. Yet they think, "If we can just get that person, then our youth problems will be solved." In the short term, they may be right, but they are wrong if they want an authentic, long-term youth ministry. Only by basing ministry on solid principles will the church begin to know the joy of a long-term, high-impact ministry to and with adults that overflows into a long-term, high-impact ministry to and with youth.

See Your Youth Ministry Through New Eyes

Throughout this book, I will be laying the groundwork that will help you establish a vital youth ministry in your church. I believe that much of what is presented here will appear to be common sense. That said, just as it is pure common sense to know that weight loss and weight control are about eating smaller portions and having a regular exercise routine, how many of us try to do something that shortcuts the natural process?

Before you move on to Chapter Two, I want to challenge you to look at your youth ministry through new eyes. See it in the context of the overall ministry of your church. Consider the dreams and hopes you have for your youth group. Can you see these same dreams and hopes for the ministry to and with the adults in your church? If you can see the big picture, you are already on your way to building a youth ministry that will go the distance. I believe the principles in this book to be so vitally important that if they are lacking in a local congregation, no youth ministry program or model will ever have lasting value.

Now What?

1. What is the state of your current youth ministry? On a scale of one to ten, how would you rate your youth ministry (with one being "We have a youth group," and ten being "Our teens are on fire for Jesus Christ")?

1	2	3	4	5	6	7	8	9	10

   Have a youth group   On fire for Jesus

2. Why did you rate the youth ministry as you did? If you rated it high, what indicates to you that the teens are "on fire?" If you rated it low, what indicates that the teens are coming just because it is expected?

_____

_____

_____

_____

3. If you are reading and studying this book with others, talk about how each person rated your youth ministry and why they rated it the way they did. If you are not reading with others, consider taking some informal surveys to get people's ratings and the reasons for them. What are you learning from others?

_____

_____

_____

_____

_____

4. Look again at the theme of this chapter and book. *"If a church is experiencing an anemic youth ministry, then the source is the overall spiritual anemia suffered within the entire church."* How does this theme ring true for you?

_____

_____

_____

_____

5. How did others who are reading this book react to this theme? Again, if you are not involved in a study group, ask members in the church, and write down their reactions.

_____

_____

_____

_____

_____

_____

6. How can you begin to strategize on increasing the spiritual vitality of the adults in your congregation?

_____

_____

_____

_____

Chapter Two
Principle #1

A healthy youth ministry flows from an intentional ministry of faith formation to and with adults.

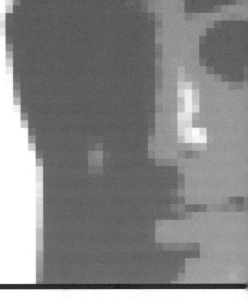

I n the introduction I claimed that the connection between a healthy youth ministry and a healthy adult ministry is just common sense. It makes so much sense that whenever I say it to youth ministry teams, people nod their heads, contemplating this connection for the first time. Even pastors, with all their seminary training and skill development, often tell me that they've never really thought about this connection.

Here is the truth: your church's intentional ministry to and with adults will be the fertile soil from which your youth ministry will grow. There is no way around this principle. If the goal is to have a long-term, successful ministry to and with youth, the congregation must get serious about developing intentional strategies for discipling adults.

This all comes down to a simple rule on which this principle-centered approach to youth ministry is based. It is a rule of congregational life that I have discovered to be true. *The spiritual growth of the youth is in direct proportion to the spiritual growth of the adults.*

If we have a church where adults are being discipled, where adults are learning how to share their faith, and where adults are engaged in passionate worship, we will have the substance from which a vital, authentic ministry to and with youth will emerge. This rule is so central that I will not even begin work on a youth consultation until I have the commitment of the pastoral staff and lay leadership that they will engage the congregation in a survey that assesses their particular strengths and weaknesses.

What is the point of offering a few ideas to a youth ministry team if worship is not passionate and inspiring to teens? We might be able to help an area here or there, but if we do not examine the whole, our impact will be minimal and our success rate low. As the youth ministry team applies new principles, they must be assisted and supported by the worship team in developing a service that can be felt and experienced.

Hey, we all know those churches where an effective youth staff person is seeing results, who actually has teens developing in faith. Yet we also know that this effective youth person will eventually leave that church. When that happens, the effectiveness of the youth ministry program will drop off because the youth ministry has been built around the person's abilities, rather than on the foundation of a strong faith community.

That youth leader may have a deep spiritual connection, but the key concern for creating a long-term, authentic youth ministry is whether the adults in the church are developing their own deep spiritual connections. If so, the youth minister will enhance the ministry of the overall church; if not, the chances for a long-term impact are greatly diminished.

The Gimmicks Were Not Working!

Early in my consultation ministry, I wanted to believe that if we gave the youth ministry team the right tools and ideas, it could build a strong youth ministry that the church would own. Outside of the occasional church with a gifted youth leader (or team), the results of giving the "right" tools and ideas were just not producing results.

I even began to redesign my training modules. I added new ideas and worked harder on my presentations because I believed that if I just taught things the right way, the youth leader (or team) would be able to build an effective, long-term youth ministry plan. Yet the results nearly always continued to be the same: the gimmicks and ideas never achieved a lasting impact on the team's youth ministry.

Well, I am not insane. Doing the same thing and receiving the same results made me stop to consider what was really going on in these churches. Perhaps the problem was not in the kind of training I provided. Perhaps it was not about the youth leader(s) not having particular skills. Perhaps it was something about the entire church. Perhaps there was a connection between what was happening with adults and what was happening—or, more often, *not* happening—with teens. I started to look at this connection, and that is when I began to see the critical foundational issues addressed in this book.

A New Approach

Believe it or not, this whole concept began to hit me when I was watching my children during their karate class. Here they were, eight and six years old, in a class of about twenty-five other eight- and six-year-olds. You should have seen them—they all looked so cute in their little karate outfits. I wondered what in the world these instructors could do to: 1) get my kid's attention, and 2) keep it.

The instructors were men and women who had achieved their black belts, and they ranged in age from twelve to sixty-plus. The fact that they had all achieved their black belts signified to the parents watching—and to the children—that these were committed people. They were qualified to teach our children because they had mastered the art of karate. You could see in their faces that these instructors loved what they did. They had genuine warmth and a sense of compassion for the children in their class.

These instructors were awesome! They would take time with each child to ensure that his or her stance was correct, that hands were in correct placement, and that the body was in proper alignment. There was no yelling or bad attitude as the instructors continued to work gently with the students who could not yet master the stance.

Not only were they gentle and compassionate, but they also held out certain expectations, beginning with the single rule that while in class, the students would not speak unless they had a question or a comment related to the instruction. Finally, the instructors held out the high expectation that students were to grow in their understanding of karate so that they could pass their proficiency tests. They encouraged and moved the class toward fulfilling the requirements that would progress it to the next level.

The instructors' expectations were not demanding, but they were a natural outgrowth of their love of karate. Their expectations emerged from a sincere desire to help children understand how they too could grow to love a sport that disciplines the body, mind, and spirit. Their expectations grew out of being the beneficiary of a system that had guided them to reaching a high level of proficiency. After the lesson, the instructors acknowledged the work each student had done, regardless of whether the child had perfected the lesson. Then the instructors would speak with the parents to offer input about their children's progress and advice on how to help them. They continually conveyed to the students the importance of practicing their skills, but not to the neglect of their schoolwork.

The whole point of the practice was to help the children learn karate, to love karate, and to advance in the sport. When it came time for advancement, if the students passed their tests, there was a special ritual for them. During the ritual, the children advancing would receive recognition for their work. Those students who did not pass were recognized for the effort they had made and were encouraged to continue learning in order to pass next time.

As I continued to watch over a number of weeks, I began to think about how this activity related to the church, to youth ministry, and even to Sunday school. My kids loved going to karate! They would come home from school and ask us when they could go. They would talk about their instructors (one was a twelve-year-old boy), and they would run to get ready when we told them that it was almost time to go. They were really into karate!

I wish I could say the same for their desire to go to Sunday school. (This is a problem when Dad is a pastor!) What was different between going to karate and going to Sunday school? What caused them to be excited about going to karate class, where workouts were not easy and expectations were high? Why couldn't they wait to go? Why did they jump to change their clothes when we said it was time to go to karate?

I was blown away that we could not create this same level of enthusiasm for going to church on Sunday morning. It fact, and I hate to admit this, but it was getting increasingly difficult for them to want to go to church and thus, increasingly difficult for us to get them to go to church.

The Adult Leaders Are the Key

My reflection on their karate experience began to give me some clues about why they loved going. I began to see how the church might build a ministry that could capture the hearts and imaginations of our children and youth.

Let's examine what the karate students experienced. They had:
- *teachers passionate about teaching the sport.* Why were they passionate about it? Because they themselves had a love of it, and their

love caused them to be passionate about teaching it to others. They were teaching what they loved and knew.

- *teachers who had already gained experience and expertise in what they were teaching* by going through the same tests and rituals that they were guiding the children through. They were not just teachers; they were practitioners.
- *teachers who were able to evaluate progress* because they had spent years practicing what they were teaching. Our children's twelve-year-old black-belt instructor had been practicing karate since the age of four. All their training and involvement had given these instructors the ability to see things that the untrained eye could not.
- *teachers who had expectations* that students would listen and develop. Think of that—what an unusual concept! They had the audacity to expect their students to develop! They believed that if the students would listen, practice, and concentrate, they too would increase their skills, knowledge, and love of the sport.
- *teachers who were willing to communicate with parents* to build up support and assistance for the children. The teachers knew that it would take the families' support for the students to advance. They knew that by including the families in the process, they were providing another tool to reinforce the things learned in class. In addition, by including the families, the teachers were building relationships of trust. They knew that parents needed to have confidence in what the teachers were doing, and they worked at building that trust.
- *teachers who were ready and willing to assist the child in moving to the next level.* They never pushed any student beyond what that student was ready to do. These teachers were awesome in that they were able to determine the learning style of students, so those who could take more assertive instruction were given it, and those who needed gentle nudging were given that. How could they do this with so many students? By maintaining a ratio of about one instructor to every five students. The goal for all the students was the same: pass the test. The way each student arrived at that test, however, was uniquely individual.
- *teachers who provided a ceremony to mark the successful completion of a skills test.* This would mark another step toward earning a black belt. The ritual proved that they were making progress, and it

was done publicly with words of encouragement and applause from those in attendance. The students knew they were on a journey, and they were encouraged by the benchmarks along the way.

Wow! As I looked at all these qualities, I was like, "This is awesome!" I also started to see why my children probably did not like going to Sunday school. I had to ask these difficult questions:

- Do we share these same qualities in the church? In what ways?
- Are our Sunday school teachers passionate about their faith in Jesus Christ? How do we know?
- Are they sharing out of their experience? Again, how do we know?
- Are our teachers able to evaluate progress? In most Sunday school programs, progress is not even a factor! We advance people based on grade and age, rather than on mastering any level of content.
- Do Sunday school teachers expect students to listen and develop in their faith journeys? They may have hopes, but do they have any expectations?
- How often do our teachers communicate with parents about the progress they see in their students' faith journeys? We have been taking our children to Sunday school for over ten years now, and in all that time, not one Sunday school teacher has been able to provide an assessment to us concerning the spiritual development of our children. I do not blame them at all; it is simply not expected of those who teach classes.
- How capable are our teachers of assisting our children in taking the next step of faith?
- How do we celebrate a student's continued progress along the journey? Sure, we have confirmation, but what do we offer to children who are able to memorize the Lord's Prayer or the Apostle's Creed? What ceremony do we have to mark a person's successful completion of a service project?

Way too often, if we are honest, we will realize that Sunday school has morphed into something that we feel needs to be done, rather than a key component of faith formation and instruction. When was the last time a mainline church ever required its potential Sunday school teachers to show any degree of faith development? In fact, it is rare for a mainline church to have any kind of standard requirement for Sunday school teachers. Face it: most churches are just happy to have someone willing to teach Sunday school.

Strange, But True

Nearly every year, I hear stories of churches that cannot "get" anyone to teach this or that class. They hope that someone, anyone, will volunteer before the session begins. It is as if anyone, as long as they have a pulse, would be acceptable to teach a class. (We will cover this in more depth in a later chapter.)

The amazing thing is that usually, someone does volunteer to pick up the class, and everyone heaves a sigh of relief that the class can go on. Regardless of whether a person is qualified or not, regardless of whether he or she has a calling or not, we really only care that the class has a teacher. We can feel good about that!

Whether it is taking our children to karate, allowing our son to play football, or putting our daughter into a drama class, we have certain expectations concerning the instructors and coaches. You see, we think that that instructors and coaches have a level of proficiency that gives them the authority and the right to teach.

Can you imagine seeing an ad in the paper that said something like, "Help Wanted: The high school football team is without coaches this year. If you are willing to coach, please call the district office. No experience or knowledge of the game is necessary." I doubt that would be in your local newspaper, but this type of thing happens every year in churches all across our nation when it is time to recruit Sunday school teachers.

What is even more amazing is that parents leave their children at church in the hands of teachers they may or may not know—and who may or may not have any particular expertise in faith formation—to study curriculum they have not reviewed, to get results they never see! It's crazy! Nowhere else are children and teenagers left to instructors who know so little about what they are teaching.

OK, there is a difference in that I am paying for those karate lessons. I want my children to learn something. I want them to grow in their understanding, and I want to witness their progress in the sport to ensure that my financial commitment is a worthwhile investment. Part of the issue in the church, though, is that parents may not even know what progress in faith formation looks like because they were never given the tools to help them in their own spiritual journeys. Unlike my ability to witness my children's karate instruction, parents do not usually take the opportunity to witness their children's Sunday school instruction. And to think that church after church wonders why their Sunday schools are not vital and exciting for our children and teens.

Sunday school teachers do not have to be biblical scholars or experts in ancient languages, but they do need to be on journeys themselves. Their teaching emerges from their continued spiritual journeys.

I know that there are many, many good and kind teachers in Sunday schools and youth ministries throughout the country. I do not mean what I say here to include the countless number of people who sacrifice in order to be there for children and youth on Sunday mornings when no one else will. These are people for whom we give thanks. In mainline churches, however, it is likely that children and teens do not get to experience the kind of passionate instruction that I saw being given by karate instructors, coaches in youth sports, and leaders of high school marching bands.

Why is all of this even important? Why am I making this such an issue? Because it relates to our ability to develop high-impact, authentic youth ministries. To ensure our youth's faith formation, we need to equip their instructors with a style of teaching that is passionate, experiential, and authentic. This is difficult when adults have had little instruction in practical faith formation. Our children and teens are not blind to what is going on in their Sunday school classes and youth rooms. They may not be able to articulate it, but they can intuit whether a teacher is passionate about a topic. They can clearly see when someone is filling a role instead of a calling. They know the difference between a lesson to be taught and a lesson to be lived.

The Bottom Line

What should be understood here, the bottom line if you will, is that unless we have an intentional approach to discipling adults, we will not have the adult faith community from which to draw empowered spiritual teachers for our youth. I believe that this principle is so critical that I have come to see a direct correlation between the spiritual lives of teens in a church and the spiritual lives of the adults in that same church.

Just because there is a correlation does not necessarily mean that there is causation, but over the years I have seen enough to believe that the spiritual development of our teens is in direct proportion to the spiritual development of our adults. Meaning this: if our adults are developing as faithful disciples through Bible studies, prayer groups, covenant groups, service teams, small-group ministries, faith-sharing initiatives, vital worship, and so forth, their development will have a tremendous impact on the viability of a ministry to and with youth.

It is critical to remember that we cannot separate youth ministry from the overall ministry of the church. One affects the other; it is all interconnected.

When I see a church where the youth ministry is stagnate, dry, and dull, I am able to make an educated guess that I am not only looking at the youth ministry, but in truth, I am looking at a mirror image of the state of the entire church. You may be saying, "Hey, that's a little tough, don't you think?"

It may sound that way, but think about how sensible this is. If youth ministry is not thriving, if teens are bored, and if they do not see any connection between faith and the real world, that is a symptom of something else going on in the church. If the adults in that church were honest, they would say they too are often bored and rarely see a connection between what they experience in church and what they experience in the real world.

Don't ever forget that vital, authentic youth ministry begins as an outgrowth of a healthy spiritual community. It is essential that we understand this connection, or we will end up trying to correct a symptom when in fact, the entire organism is in need of being examined.

During a consultation, I usually ask people to share their hopes and dreams for their youth ministry. In nearly every church, the most common statements I hear are that they want the teens to study the Bible, they want them to pray, they want them to be able to share their faith with others, and they want them to invite their friends to church. These church leaders understand what they want, but they do not know how to get there.

So I affirm all their hopes and dreams, but then I ask if the adults are involved in Bible study. Are they in prayer groups or covenant groups? When was the last time they shared their faith? And when was the last time they invited someone to church?

Please understand that I do not ask these questions to be an "in your face" type of guy, but I want them to begin the process of opening their eyes. I always hope that they will be able to come to the realization that what they do not see happening in their youth ministry is a mirror image of what is not happening in the adult ministry. Thus, they are expanding their vision by looking at the needs of the entire church. By finding the courage to look in the mirror, they are able to discover for themselves that the hopes and dreams they have for the youth are the hopes and dreams they really have for their entire church.

Responsible Role Models

By definition, adults are role models of the faith. For better or for worse, every adult in every church serves as an example to children and teens of what it means to be a Christian man or woman.

.This is not just something that happens. Every time there is a baptism, the faith community as a whole and as individuals promises to live their lives in such a way that they will be Christian role models for the child as he or she grows up among them.

Doesn't that blow you away? We promise to help this child understand the faith by seeking to live our lives after Christ! That is a pretty heavy responsibility for adults in the church. The community of faith is absolutely called to live out the African proverb that reminds us, "It takes a village to raise a child."

Yet if the promise is to become more than just a nice part of a baby's baptism ritual, adults must begin to deepen and develop their intentional process of faith formation. The fact that we make this promise should cause us to seek out how God is calling us to live our discipleship and be faithful in this world. If I take seriously my promise and carry my responsibility for that child, then I need to be serious about this journey of faith. If I want that child to experience the power of a journey into the heart of God, then I need to have the courage to take the journey myself.

Let me be clear. Even adults who never teach a class or lead a youth study have a part in the faith formation of the children and teens in their church. Just because we do not teach or lead others does not release us from the responsibility of ordering our lives in such a way that makes us examples of faith for the children and teens in our church.

Ultimately, we have to ask, "If adults do not share their faith, if they are not involved in Bible study, and if they are not inviting people to worship, why would our children and teens do anything more?" It is essential that we look in the mirror—that we have the courage to fearlessly evaluate who we are as a community of faith. What is it about the way we live out our faith that encourages teens and children to join us on this journey?

Remember the karate instructors? They not only wanted the students to learn, but they themselves were ongoing practitioners of the art. They did not just tell the students what to do, they did not just prepare a lesson, and they did not just download something from the Internet. They taught by demonstration, which was born out of their own years of study and practice. The students paid attention because the teachers demonstrated themselves to be people the students could learn from just by watching. The students learned to value their instructors' teachings because their instructors were teaching from their own practice and experience.

Consider another example. When our children were little, my wife and I wanted them to value reading, so we read to them. Not only did we read to them, but we intentionally read at such times and in such places that they would see us with books, magazines, and newspapers in our hands. Even before they could read, we always encouraged them whenever they picked up a book.

When they became older, we began having them read to us. Over the years, we successfully developed in our children the value and importance of reading. We did this by modeling, encouraging, and supporting them in their efforts. Even now, we continue to model the importance of reading to gain knowledge and understanding and to have an alternative form of entertainment. Here is the secret: in order for reading to become valuable to our children, my wife and I needed to first value it in our lives.

In the same way, if we want our youth to value the spiritual journey, we need to be a church that is intentionally on that journey. If we do not grab hold of this value, then what are we passing on? What are we actually sharing by being role models? Do we want our children and teens to be passionate about the Gospel? Do we want them to know the value of God in their lives?

If we do, and most congregations I visit do, then we need to live it out by first and foremost allowing these signs of discipleship to become values for us. We cannot depend on one or two or even a small group of people to pass on these values to our teens. They may succeed on occasion, but a high-impact, long-term, authentic youth ministry requires an effort on the part of every adult to take seriously the life we have been called to live in Christ Jesus.

It's Hard Work!

This is hard work! It is a heavy responsibility. Are you up for it? I hope so, because we have more churches teaching children and teens how to be "good" church members than how to live passionately the beautiful life we have been given in Christ Jesus. That really is our choice—either we live as passionate expressions of the love of God in this world, or we settle for teaching children and teens how to "do" church.

We already know that many young adults and Baby Boomers are not interested in just doing church, in just keeping the doors open, or in just helping the church with its committee work. If we are going to reach this generation and call back a lost generation, we must regain our passion for Bible study, prayer, service, worship, and faith-sharing. We need to be adults who are seeking to live out these values in our daily lives. We need to allow the passion and the power of our spiritual lives to become real and authentic to us before it will become real and authentic to the next generation.

That is the bottom line for children and teens: they want to know if what we say is real, and they want to know if we are authentic in what we say. We can say we believe something, but do we live as though we believe? We can say something has value, but do we live as though it has value?

We are not talking about being perfect here. We are talking about being adults on intentional spiritual journeys seeking to assist others with their journeys. Do not ever forget that we cannot lead someone to go where we ourselves have not yet been. Good teachers know and accept this and, to ensure their students' progress, help them discover a new teacher who can take them even further along the journey.

Simply put, in churches where there is an intentional approach to adult faith formation, there is, without a doubt, more opportunity to build a long-term, effective, and authentic youth ministry. When adults are growing in faith, their growth adds a great deal of support and stability to every area of the church. When this is happening, the adults in these churches see themselves as partners in the youth pastor's ministry, rather than the youth pastor working on behalf of the church. These adults grasp the full understanding that worship is not just something nice to attend, but rather the weekly expression of our shared faith journey in Christ.

Can you see what a different way of thinking this is? And how sensible it is? Understanding this initial principle—a healthy youth ministry flows from an intentional ministry of faith formation to and with adults—is the basis for understanding everything laid out in this book.

In order to share, teach, partner, or build a youth ministry team, adults need to have passion for, knowledge of, and experience in the spiritual life. I say again emphatically that adults do not have to be perfect or have all the answers, but they do need to be intentionally on the journey. This principle is the foundation, and if is not in place, then your congregation will continue to struggle with starts and stops in youth ministry. Your congregation will continue to seek the "ideal" youth minister or to attempt the latest fad, only to realize that the results are just not being sustained.

Are you ready to gather a group of people to fearlessly and courageously evaluate your church? Are you ready to get serious about building a foundation for youth ministry that will be stronger than you ever imagined possible? Then work through the questions that follow.

Now What?

In order to move toward meaningful youth ministry, we have to be willing to face our current reality and avoid the trap of a vision that does not exist. Do not misunderstand me. Feelings are important, and we do not want to hurt people unnecessarily, but we are talking about having an effective youth ministry that prepares our teens to be disciples in this world. In order to do this, we need to be able to look in the mirror and see who and what we are as a faith community. We need to be able to evaluate whether we are actively pursuing faith formation for adults and whether it is a core value from which everything else emerges.

1. On a scale of 1 to 10, rate the adult discipleship program in your church.

   1   2   3   4   5   6   7   8   9   10
   Adults come to worship   Fired up and growing

   Talk with others about the reasons for your answers. If you rate your church an "8," then tell the group why and where you see your church fired up and growing. If someone else rates the church a "2," then the reality is probably going to be somewhere in between. Through your discussion with others, you may begin to uncover how different people understand faith formation differently.

_____

_____

_____

_____

2. List the discipleship-building ministries in your church (adult Bible studies, prayer groups, evangelism training, and so forth). What percentage of adults would you say are involved in these classes?

_____

_____

_____

_____

3. Ask the pastor and staff whether there is a strategic faith-formation plan in place that is meant to inspire growth and passion in the adult members of your congregation. Write the response below.

_____

_____

_____

_____

_____

4. On a scale of 1 to 10, rate the value of Bible study in your church.

1   2   3   4   5   6   7   8   9   10

Low   High

What evidence do you have to support your answer? Be careful here, because we may value Bible study and still not engage in Bible study. If you rate the value a "9," but there are only 15 percent of adults involved in Bible study classes, what other indicators do you have that lead you to believe that Bible study is highly valued?

_____

_____

_____

_____

_____

5. On a scale of 1 to 10, rate the value of prayer in your church.

1	2	3	4	5	6	7	8	9	10
Low									High

Why did you answer the way you did? What evidence do you have?

_____

_____

_____

_____

6. On a scale of 1 to 10, rate your church's value on service to the community (feeding the poor, prison ministries, reaching out to the neighborhood, and so forth).

1	2	3	4	5	6	7	8	9	10
Low									High

Why did you give the answer that you did? What evidence do you have to support this rating?

_____

_____

_____

_____

People often feel defeated right about now because the illusions they have created about their church do not match reality. I encourage you *not* to feel defeated if you are scoring low on these questions, but to be inspired that by dropping the illusions, you can start to create an environment where adult faith formation is taken seriously. I know that you are reading this book because you are concerned about youth ministry, but the foundation for a strong, high-impact, long-term youth ministry begins with this principle.

Your pastor will be your greatest asset. He or she is probably eager to have laypeople on board who understand the need for adult faith formation. Ask your pastor to talk about his or her hopes and dreams for the church. Ask about ideas to increase the value of faith formation among adults. Begin to support and encourage the pastor to be the spiritual leader God called him or her to be. Ignite his or her passion of guiding adults into a deeper expression of discipleship. Just by beginning to work on this with your pastor, you will have already strengthened the foundation of your youth ministry.

Chapter Three
Principle #2

*A healthy youth ministry understands
the positive expression
of teen empowerment.*

I n Chapter One, we looked at how the youth ministry may be reflective of the overall church ministry. In Chapter Two, we examined the need to be intentional about adult faith formation in order for teens to witness adults who are seeking to model the faith in daily living. If the hope and dream is to see teens grow in faith, then they need to be surrounded by adults who are intentionally developing their own faith journeys.

This chapter will build on Chapter Two by looking at one of the most abused and misunderstood philosophies of current youth ministry: the concept of teen empowerment, or teens leading teens. This great concept has now become, in some cases, not at all what it was intended to be. I want to be clear from the beginning that I am a proponent of teen empowerment; however, I believe that teen empowerment is to be set within certain parameters that we will explore in this chapter. This principle is closely related to Principle #1 in that we will never have true teen empowerment until we have an intentional process of adult faith formation.

Empowered Teens

Understood and practiced correctly, teen empowerment is a philosophy of youth ministry that can build a strong core of teen leaders who will not only have an impact on the youth ministry, but also on the total ministry of the congregation. Teen empowerment is too critical to the overall mission of the congregation to be haphazardly employed. Yet that is exactly what happens when a cultural understanding of empowerment overtakes the spiritual meaning of true empowerment. The potential for true teen empowerment is huge, but it can be reduced if empowerment is misunderstood. Before we jump into how youth empowerment has been misused or misunderstood, though, let's begin with defining the most positive ideal of what it can be and how it can benefit the overall mission of the church.

Ideally, teen empowerment is about teens leading, designing, and implementing a ministry strategy that reaches teens, impacts the ministry of the congregation, and reaches out to the community and the world. It has the potential not only to impact teens, but also to profoundly affect the lives of adults. Now that is a high calling for teen empowerment!

When we use this positive description as our building block for teen empowerment, it becomes apparent that empowerment takes place when teens begin to awaken spiritually to the reality of who they are and what they are called to be as disciples of Jesus Christ. True teen empowerment takes place as a result of a teen's willingness to enter into a process of faith formation. It is through this process that a teen comes to realize that God has called him or her to be in ministry to and with the faith community. Empowerment is something that one awakens to during an intentional journey of spiritual formation.

Adults become essential to the awakening process in the life of a child or teen. As these awakening, empowered teens grasp the totality and meaning of the mission of the church, they become partners with adults in reaching the world for Christ. When this ideal growth happens, teen empowerment affects the local church in ways that contribute significantly to the overall mission of the church. These are the teens who get it—they get who they are as disciples of Jesus Christ, and they get that their ministry is far more than planning and having activities for people their age.

To be an empowered teen is to be a teen who is spiritually awakening and becoming a critical part of moving God's message of liberation in this world. When teens are empowered in this way, they become vital partners on all local church boards and agencies. They are instrumental in the entire ministry because their spiritual gifts are realized, celebrated, and put into the strategy of the overall mission.

I have had the extreme pleasure of being in ministry with teens who are empowered in this way. I have witnessed the power of sharing in ministry with teens who literally became partners in ministry. I have seen teens experience the true empowerment of the Spirit to the extent that, given the opportunity, they had the tools to lead faith-formation programs and activities for adults.

I will never forget one experience I had while in ministry with a group of teen leaders from throughout our East Ohio Conference. (Each year, the Lord just blows me away by allowing me to experience the level of faith development in these teens' lives.) I was given the opportunity to lead a training session for adults on youth ministry. I thought it might set a good working model if I brought one of our teen leaders with me to share and assist in the workshop. What unfolded was something I never expected.

For nearly two full sessions, we took a tag-team approach to talking with adults about how to be in ministry to and with youth. What we actually did became far more effective than what we were talking about doing. My teen partner and I literally worked off each other and picked up where the other left off. As a team, we showed that teens and adults can be effective doing ministry together.

Unfortunately, many teens do not get the opportunity to have this kind of experience. All too often, teens get discouraged because they feel as though they are not being heard and that that their gifts are not being utilized. I tend to agree with these teens, but not because they are being held out of the process of empowerment. The fact that they are not being heard or utilized is not due to a grand conspiracy, but rather to adults not understanding how to engage and guide youth to involvement in the overall mission and ministry of the church. If adults are not intentionally on the spiritual journey, then how can they empower teens who want to be on that journey?

When a church is focused on maintaining itself rather than on actively pursuing its mission, there is not a lot of enthusiasm from the adults for the level of passion, excitement, and commitment that can come from teens. Think about it. If adults are not really sure about their own faith journeys, they will be scared to death of teens who want to get serious about theirs.

Adults who are actively involved with teens, who are focused on the primary task of the church, and who understand the nature of true empowerment will enter into a shared ministry with teens—a ministry that will benefit both teens and adults as they seek to be faithful to God's calling.

I will never forget the day our regional teen executive board was working on one of our key weekend spiritual-life events. We had literally outgrown the facility we had been using for four years; however, I was fine with keeping the event there. It was a comfortable venue for me because I knew the convention center crews, and over the years I had built relationships with the hotels. I also knew that many of the churches that came were familiar our setting, and a change in venue could have had a negative impact on attendance. I was even OK with limiting the size of the event to what the venue could hold, but it quickly became apparent that this was not OK with our teen executive team.

The team was simply not satisfied with keeping the event where it was, and not just because they wanted the event to get bigger. One of the officers spoke up and said, "If this event is about reaching teens and adults for Jesus Christ, then we have to have it in a location where all who want to come are able to attend and participate. No person should be shut out from attending because we ran out of seats."

It was in that moment that I realized that God had been empowering these teens to know what their highest calling was. It was then that we became partners in ministry; I knew that they were right, and I knew we would be taking a step in faith to go to a new venue.

Because they were getting connected in the heart of the Spirit, they were able to challenge me to move beyond my comfort zone and seek the Lord on what we were really being called to do. Through prayer, the Spirit led me to trust in what these teens wanted to do.

What a powerful example of teen empowerment! Teens willing to listen to the Spirit, do whatever it took to reach others, and step out in faith. They blew me away, and in that instance, God used them to teach me a lesson in faith.

It is important to note that these teen leaders are part of an ongoing process that teaches them the value of being servant leaders. They are part of an accountability group, where they are able to express and share the spiritual-formation activities they have experienced between meetings. The adult leaders set the standard by modeling and continually sharing the attributes of being servant leaders while guiding the teens to the purpose of why we do what we do. By challenging us to move to a venue that would reach more teens, these leaders got it. They understood that our mission was to spread the good news in all that we did, and if that meant a bigger facility, so be it. Because of their faith and commitment, these teens were able to challenge the adults to get it too. This is teen empowerment at its best.

Wow! Isn't this a cool concept? Think about it. Empowered teens able to share in the ministry to be liberators for Jesus Christ in a world full of those enslaved and oppressed in so many ways (spiritually, culturally, politically, and so forth). These empowered teens were fantastic to have actively involved themselves in ministry plans as partners with adults to reach the world for Jesus Christ.

When both teens and adults are empowered in this way, a powerful ministry team is built. There is a free flow of ideas—there are no worries about who is in charge or who gets to make decisions. When teens feel this kind of empowerment and are engaged in trusting relationships with adults who care about and walk with them, they experience empowerment of the Spirit in such a way that they will never be the same—and neither will the adults who share ministry with them. The church will be transformed as a result of empowered teens calling it to a deeper level of faithfulness.

When Empowerment Is No More Than a Voice and a Vote

Sounds good, right? This is the kind of empowerment you want for your teens, right? So with such a cool philosophy for youth ministry, what's the problem?

The problem is that what you have just read is simply the ideal and rarely the practice of youth empowerment. This totally powerful concept of teen empowerment usually gets boiled down to, in all practicality, teens having a voice and a vote within the church power structure. This is especially true in the area of youth ministry, where teen empowerment has come to be taken as teens getting to decide what their youth program will be and how the meeting will take place.

In addition, a church may feel that teens are empowered if they serve on church committees and have the right to vote in church councils. In fact, most of the teen advocacy that I hear in my denomination is all about getting teens named to committees so that they have a voice throughout the church political structure.

Even in the youth ministry itself, teens are considered empowered if they get to map out their own calendar and decide when they are having this or that fundraiser. Often, adult leaders believe that just allowing teens to lead their own ministry without providing specific guidance is the way to allow them to be empowered. Where did this come from?

OK, so we take this cool concept of teen empowerment and break it down to having teens sit on committees and vote on where the annual church picnic will be held. That's empowerment?

If your church is like many I have visited, the standing committees are filled with good people who basically support the current way of doing things, regardless of whether their ministry is reaching the world or strengthening its members' spiritual lives. Even though there may be good and kind people on these committees, the committees are not the places I want teens to be simply so that they have a voice and a vote.

As our teens learn the depth of empowerment, we need to be careful that they do not simply settle for learning how to become good church committee people. Empowerment will not come simply because youth get to vote on a committee. That is a minimalist way of dealing with empowerment, and it will have little, if any, effect on empowering youth to help the church fulfill its mission of carrying God's message of salvation to the world.

Seriously, why would I want teens to be part of something where they will learn absolutely nothing more than how to be "good" church people and keep the church maintained? Why would I want them to be part of a decision-making process that is more about "our" church than it is about being the Church of Jesus Christ? Why would I want teens to be subjected to committees that are comfortable with their church, rather than actively seeking to be liberators in a world of oppression? We can put teens on boards, but it will take a good deal of prayer and guidance to keep them from getting bored, frustrated, and indoctrinated into a style of church that is not producing results.

This popular understanding of teen empowerment (that is, getting them a voice and a vote) is not empowerment at all, but rather enslavement. It is enslavement to a structure and a political system that have, at best, a minimal impact on the world. Some might argue that placing teens on these boards and committees will help them feel as if the church values them. Perhaps, but I think that we can help them find more appropriate and effective ways to feel valuable than having to sit on church committees that do a lot of talking but little reaching out to a hurting world.

Let's be honest. How many of you right now are getting bored with the mere idea of being on a church committee? (I know I am.) So here is a tough concept—one that goes against pop culture.

Our job in being in a ministry to and with youth is not about helping teens feel important. Rather, it is about helping teens experience the power of God in their lives, helping them realize that God values them, and letting them know that God has given them gifts that will help others know God. When these things happen, teens will automatically feel important because they will be part of something that is vitally important. Teens will also feel important when spiritually developing adults invest time and care in their lives. That investment, that care, that compassion, and that listening ear will empower teens in a far greater, more profound way than serving on any traditional church committee will ever do. As we share in ministry with teens, they will gain voice and vote, they will gain respect, and they will gain confidence in their ability to be used by God.

Be careful now. I am in no way indicating that we should keep teens from being on church committees or involved in the church structure. In fact, as we are moving toward our understanding of true empowerment, this practice will become a must. I find, however, that most standing committees and councils in established congregations have one priority, and that is to maintain the status quo.

Now don't get mad at me for telling the truth. All too many mainline churches fail to see that their active role is to function as a mission outpost for Jesus Christ and as a center of spiritual formation for people seeking to deepen their faith. If our traditional churches had cutting-edge committees actively pursuing the mission and ministry of Jesus Christ, then the state of mainline churches would not be as fragile as it currently is, now, would it? We would not have such a struggle reaching teens, and we would not find ourselves on the margin of cultural relevancy.

So be sure to take that courageous self-evaluation, and look in that mirror. See whether the committees in your congregation are actively moving the church's primary mission forward. If they are, get the teens on those committees ASAP! It is here that teens will witness empowered adults. Here teens will be challenged, and they will experience firsthand adults who get that the purpose of the church is to make disciples.

When teens are part of these inspired committees, they meet adults who realize that God is able to speak through all people. The adults *lis-*

ten to the youth because they believe that God speaks through teens as readily as God speaks through adults, and, as a result, the teens will feel truly empowered by the faith community.

I believe that discipled teens can be extremely powerful instruments of God's redemptive work. They have a level of passion, excitement, and inspiration that comes from being totally committed to a cause for which they see real need, real impact, and real results. This youth-driven excitement is sometimes too much for "good" church people to handle, but in churches where the supreme value is in reaching the least, the last, and the lost, the passion that teens bring to the table will inspire everyone on the committee. Their passionate call to be faithful to the church's core values will encourage and challenge adult members to continue developing effective strategies that reach the world for Jesus Christ.

These are the kinds of committees that I want to see youth involved in, because here they will serve with spiritually passionate and growing adults who will act as mentors, or spiritual friends. These mentors will assist the teens in utilizing their spiritual gifts to become disciples of Jesus Christ, thus *truly* empowering them to be active participants in God's redemptive work. These spiritual adult friends will then be able to listen to what the teen (or anyone) says and evaluate it in light of what God is calling them to be and do. When the committee is focused on the purpose of the church, any person, regardless of age or experience, becomes a vital link in God's plan. This kind of committee will lead to an overall authentic spirituality for the church—one that teens will want to be part of because the work/ministry/service is dynamic and transcendent.

Here's an example of what I mean. Most local church trustees are charged with the care of church facilities. At its best, the church building is simply a tool that a community of faith uses to serve as both a mission outpost and a training center for those seeking to follow Christ. At worst, the church becomes a monument to God built by members whose sole desire is to maintain the monument. The trustees can either ensure the tool be used for its God-given purpose, or they can perpetuate the building as a monument to be maintained—to the exclusion of doing effective ministry.

I have seen both kinds of trustees. The trustees who see the church as a mission outpost and center of spiritual formation continually find ways to utilize the facility for these purposes. The other kind of trustees feels their main priority is to protect the building, so they develop multiple policies and find ways to restrict its use.

So which group do I want serving with growing teen disciples of Jesus Christ? Obviously, it's the trustees who understand the mission of the church, as together, they will work to continue shaping the physical structure to reach people for Christ. I do not want a teen to serve on a board whose main priority is simply to maintain a building. Sure, a spiritually empowered teen can make an impact even on these types of committees, but unless the clergy and lay leaders are working to turn around the committees' spiritual core, our teens' efforts will be minimal. For committees to turn toward a functional approach to doing ministry, the church as a whole must often go through an extreme spiritual makeover.

For most teens, the issue of empowerment is most felt at the level of youth ministry. Yet many churches have taken the incredible idea of teens empowered to lead their ministry and boiled it down to teens getting to decide what to do in their ministry. If teens are part of the decision-making process, we are told they "own" the program and thus, will be more actively involved with the program. This sounds good, but it may or may not be true.

The reality is that teens are no more likely to attend a youth event planned by teens than they are to attend one planned by adults. The teens who plan the event may have more invested, but the other teens in the church do not attend based on who plans events. They attend based on the authenticity of the ministry and on the relationships being built within that ministry. Teen empowerment for ministry is not about who makes decisions or who gets on a committee. Empowerment is simply not about the church's political structure.

I run into well-meaning youth pastors all the time who are ill-advised about youth empowerment. They believe that youth empowerment is just about asking the youth what they want to do and then helping them do it. Like adults in the mainline church, teens may have little understanding of why the church exists. It is only through our relationships with teens that we will excel at providing ministries that impact lives for Jesus Christ.

Mainline churches seem to be so worried about who is at the decision table that little thought is given to whether the people at the table even understand the nature of the work they have been invited to do. I truly believe that this approach comes from good intentions.

In the depths of their hearts, most people probably realize that the church is not reaching its fullest potential. "So," they think, "if we can just get the political structure together, then someday God's reign will be realized among us." It sounds good, and it can provide some good ideas, but in the end, this approach misses the reality of what it means to be spiritually empowered disciples of Jesus Christ.

Youth Are the Leaders of Tomorrow—and Today!

The idea that the "youth do it" has created the battle cry, "Youth are not the *leaders of tomorrow*; they are the *leaders of today*!" How many of us have heard a speaker say that we need to be intentional about our ministry with teens because they will be the church leaders tomorrow, only to be instantly corrected by someone in the audience saying that teens are the leaders today? People seem to really believe they are supporting their youth when they get behind this battle cry, and more and more I just want to say, "Oh, please."

Think about it. Who will hold the primary positions of church leadership ten, twenty, or thirty years from now? For the most part, tomorrow's leaders are today's teens. The statement that youth are the leaders of tomorrow is true, and it does not demean teens.

Our town has traditionally produced very successful high school girls softball teams, and developing the players begins early in the lives of our local girls. When we see third- and fourth-grade girls playing softball, we can honestly say that out there, on that diamond, is the future of our high school team. Are they a softball team now? Of course they are, but they will only become high school players if they are dedicated to pursuing their sport. What they are learning as young girls today will prepare them for what they will encounter as they develop in the sport.

What *does* it mean to be a leader in the church today? Does just being a teen and going to church make one a leader?

In a nutshell, leadership in the church takes place when people (or committees) are guiding the church to be a center of spiritual formation and a mission outpost for Jesus Christ. Just because you have teens in the church does not mean they are leaders any more than are the adults who simply attend church. Becoming a leader is a process, not simply a right one has by virtue of being part of a group. I do not care what age a person is; if someone understands the purpose of the church and is actively seeking to live and develop as a disciple of Jesus Christ, then that person has the potential to be an effective church leader. Empowerment for ministry is about teens being an active, contributing, and vital part of the overall ministry strategy that is first and foremost about reaching the world for Jesus Christ.

I have met teens who can provide that kind of effective leadership, and I have met adult leaders who cannot. The reality is that we are all in a process today to become more effective spiritual leaders tomorrow. We all develop differently. A teen who has gone to church since birth may no more be a leader today than a teen who never goes to church; however, the former may have a future spiritual awakening based on the authentic relationships he or she experiences in church today.

The next time you hear someone say that the youth are the leaders of tomorrow, you can answer, "Yes, that is true. They are the leaders of tomorrow, but we are building a better tomorrow by guiding them to be disciples of Jesus Christ today, and some of them may even be effective church leaders today."

I am passionate about this because I have spent too many years working with adults and youth who were upset about who was getting to make decisions and not about whether their existing ministry plan was having any impact. This is exactly why I am not too interested in having teens serve on most traditional church committees and councils. Until churches are unapologetically committed to their ministry in Christ Jesus, it does not matter who makes decisions, because the impact of those decisions will not make any real difference in the long run.

Adults and Teens Working Together

I *totally* believe that teens can be empowered to plan and implement youth ministry programs and activities. I absolutely think that empowered teens can plan and implement entire church strategies. I do not believe, however, that teens have this ability just because they are teens, anymore than I think that a person can play the trumpet just because he or she owns one.

I have sat in meetings where adults fought for teens' rights to make ministry decisions without even knowing whether the teens had any of kind of spiritual life or whether they even wanted to make those kinds of decisions. Basically, they were fighting to allow the teens to have control of their own ministry simply because they were teens.

Friends, empowering teens does not mean that adults give up their responsibility and take a backseat as the youth facilitate the process. Adults should never totally abdicate to the desires and wishes of the youth, nor should young people be left to themselves to find out what it means to be a member of their community. The ideal is for adults and teens to be actively involved *together* in ministry to reach the world for Jesus Christ.

Youth ministry is about adults and teens working together. It is about teens growing, developing, and being given leadership opportunities as they grow and develop in their faith formation. Empowerment and leadership are born out of the mentoring relationship that takes place between student and teacher.

Now some of you may be saying, "Wait a minute! Are you saying adults should be in charge?" There we go again. Why are we worried about who is in charge? Being in charge is not the issue. Granted, we all know adults who have a power thing going, and they plan everything from the annual canoe trip to the weekly program without ever getting input or assistance from teens. Many of us would agree that this level of control is terrible and unacceptable.

I reject this type of leadership as much as I reject the "youth do it" approach. It is this abusive, controlling adult leadership style that has created the belief that teens need to be in charge. The power pendulum has swung toward teens just doing it, and we need to bring it back to the center.

Youth empowerment is amazing, real, and powerful when youth are coached, instructed, and walked with on their spiritual journeys. Teens who are thoughtful, who question, and who seek guidance from adult mentors begin to grow into strong, effective church leaders with the desire to seek God in all they do.

These coached teens become tremendous leaders in the cause of Jesus Christ for the church. If adults do not spiritually coach/mentor/guide (whatever you want to call it), then youth empowerment is just a PC way of getting teens superficially involved.

We need to break free of this superficiality because it is not producing results—unless we are looking for results that focus on creating good Mini-Me church people. Lord help us if all we produce are Mini-Me's. No way! I want teens to develop as leaders who are committed to bringing the life, love, and passion of Jesus into this world.

Therefore, to be truly empowered means that an individual is on an intentional spiritual journey, regardless of age. The majority of teens start this journey due to a key relationship with an adult role model (more on this in Chapter Five). As teens grow in their passion for Christ and for the redemptive work of God in this world, they begin to emerge as truly empowered disciples of Jesus Christ. They then become the leaders that the church so desperately needs during this time of cultural transition in which the church is seeking its place of relevancy.

Empowerment and Spiritual Formation

By now you should be getting that empowerment is not about who makes decisions, but it is at its core an issue of spiritual development. As I have noted before, I have the opportunity to be in ministry with a youth council of over fifty teen leaders from across our region. As we meet, we work more on spiritual formation than on leadership skills. In fact, by working on spiritual formation and sharing with one another, we are seeking to model true spiritual leadership.

We model servant leadership more than decision-making. We listen and work toward consensus more than we vote, and we seek God's direction in what we do more than we worry about who among us gets to be on stage during a planned event. Our goal is to help teens see how God is involved in their lives through the *process* of leadership, rather than focusing on who gets the leadership title, who gets to make a decision, or whose idea is accepted.

The amazing thing that we have discovered over the years is that our older teens truly become living expressions of empowerment. The adults do not have to be in front during a meeting. The adults do not have to be in front during devotionals. In fact, the adults do not have to be in front for anything, because our teen leaders have become living expressions of what it means to be empowered leaders for the cause of Jesus Christ.

Does this mean they do not need the adults? Not at all, but most of the adults' work with teen leaders happens prior to the meeting. It does mean that we have to continue being diligent in helping our teens process their spiritual lives. We have to intentionally ensure that younger teens are growing in their faith so that they too can enter the depths of empowered spiritual leadership. We will know our teen leaders are growing when they are able to empower younger teens by giving them responsibilities, as well as by asking for and listening to their input.

The adult's role is to guide, coach, encourage, and challenge the teens to be focused on the primary task in all they do. This takes diligence. The adult leaders cannot let up on their responsibilities—you are there to question, evaluate, share, and listen as teens continue to process their spiritual leadership experiences.

In my ministry, I have witnessed the powerful transformation of teens from decision-maker wannabes to disciples seeking to lead others to a deeper understanding of Jesus Christ. I have witnessed the spiritual maturation process accelerated in some teens to the point that I believe they could be spiritual guides in many mainline churches—to adults. Those are empowered teens!

I have also seen teen leaders mentor younger teens. The older teens are able to introduce the younger ones to our group's mission. They set the standards and lift up the core values as they seek to serve as examples of what it means to be in a shared ministry with adults.

Listen up, adults! All this means is *your* spiritual life counts! How you grow and develop will impact the level of true empowerment your teens experience.

Think about it. *You* have the ability to lead your teens into the fullness of spiritual empowerment! *You* have a huge responsibility to be an experienced, understanding, and passionate coach who is willing to walk with others on their journeys.

You cannot coach what you do not know or what you have not experienced. Spiritual empowerment does not just happen; it is cultivated and nurtured and guided. Teen empowerment is real, but getting there is work. Claim your role as a coach who has been given the greatest opportunity: the opportunity to guide youth into spiritual empowerment that will impact the church today and in the future.

Give Teens Support

If you have teens serving on church committees, you (or another adult mentor) can help them experience empowerment by:

- talking to them prior to meetings to see what they expect to be covered;
- asking them whether they are willing to share their feelings about particular committee issues and what they think needs to be done at the meeting;
- talking to them after the meeting to see how things went. Try to discover whether teens feel as if they were heard.

- asking teens whether they feel as if the committee is centered on the primary task of making disciples. If not, ask what they think can be done to bring the committee back to the center.
- providing teens the opportunity to vent and explore alternatives. This way, you are helping teens process the entire experience.

Now What?

1. How many teens are currently serving on committees and councils in your church?

   _____

2. Of these youth, how many are assigned to an adult to assist them in processing what is going on in the committee or council?

   _____

3. Is there a process by which you monitor teens' effectiveness on boards and councils? If so, what is it?

   _____

   _____

   _____

4. It is key to have a process by which teens debrief a committee or council on their experiences. Is there such a process? If so, is it effective? If not, what would it take to add one to your current youth ministry?

   _____

   _____

   _____

5. In what ways are teens serving as leaders for the youth ministry? Do they do more than map out a calendar of events? If so, what else do they do?

   _____

   _____

   _____

   _____

6. On a scale of one to ten (one being they know there has to be a mission, and ten meaning they totally get it and are committed to the mission and vision), how would you rate your teen leaders' ability to articulate the mission and vision of the youth ministry?

1   2   3   4   5   6   7   8   9   10
Has to be a mission   Committed to the mission

Why did you rate it the way you did? How did others rate it?

_____

_____

_____

_____

7. Ask your teens to articulate to you what they believe the mission and vision for their ministry is. Then write down what they say, and reflect on how near or far they are from the mark. If there is a wide range of answers, what does that say to you?

_____

_____

_____

_____

_____

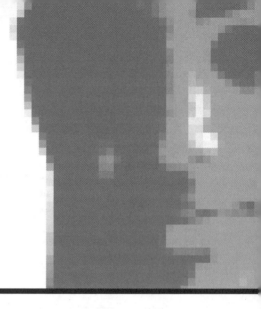

Chapter Four
Principle #3

A healthy youth ministry understands the difference between youth activity and youth ministry.

N ot long into a church youth leaders meeting, I had this exchange with one of the leaders. We will call her Elaine.

Elaine: All this material about faith sharing and building relationships is really good, but we thought you were going to tell us how to get our teens involved in church activities.

Ed: Like what kind of activities?

Elaine: Like getting them to go on canoe trips and to the amusement park, to come to church dinners, to come here for game night, and even to help with the annual church bazaar and things like that.

Ed: You would like to plan activities and get the teens to come to those activities?

Elaine: Yes!

Ed: And you want me to teach you the steps to planning a youth activity so that youth will come?

Elaine: Yes!

Ed: Why?

Elaine: So that they will be involved in the church.

Ed: Why?

Elaine: Because it is good for them and gives them an alternative to what they might be tempted to do if the church were not offering an activity.

Ed: So, you want to do activities so that the teens have something to do that is good, wholesome, safe, sponsored by the church, interesting to them, gets them involved in church life, and provides them an opportunity to do something that keeps them out of trouble?

Elaine: Exactly!

Ed: Then what?

Elaine: Well, we have another activity.

Ed: So the point of youth ministry is to continue to provide activities that are interesting, fun, and keep teens involved in church?

Elaine: Yes!

Ed: OK... .

Elaine has good intentions. She desperately wants to have a youth group connected to the church. She wants the teens "involved," and she thinks that by getting them involved in church activities, they will somehow stay out of trouble and may even learn to like church.

Elaine is lifting up the concept of an activity-driven model for youth ministry that will be successful to some extent, but, in the end, will leave her frustrated when she discovers that simply doing activities will not keep teens in church. Teens may like to do an activity and associate that good time with the church, but that does not mean they will receive or enter into deeper spiritual experiences, which are needed in order to maintain a long-term, authentic impact on their lives.

Elaine represents many of the volunteer youth leaders that I have met over the years—great people who love teens and want to see them live vital lives for Jesus Christ. Unfortunately, when these leaders cannot keep teens coming to church activities or get them to attend worship, they think they are failures. Their whole focus is on the number of teens they can get involved in activities. Becoming discouraged, they do not think they are cut out for youth ministry and end up quitting.

Or, leaders like Elaine become successful with activities, and the teens feel good about their leaders. The end result is the same, however, in that the good feelings and fun times do not necessarily develop vital spiritual experiences that lead to empowered lives having a long-term impact on the church. So either way, the activity-driven model is a one that can produce numbers but may not be able to achieve the results we are really looking for: long-term impact on the individual and the church.

The Youth-Activity Model

As I have said throughout this book, getting teens involved and keeping them connected to Christ is hard work, and there is no quick fix. An activity-driven model is usually just that—an attempt to provide a quick fix. In this chapter, we will explore why this type of model is not a good idea. Then we will look at a positive way of using activities as part of an overall strategy to deepen faith formation in the lives of teens.

When consulting, it quickly becomes apparent who wants to develop a real ministry to and with teens, and who wants to have activities. Many churches I consult with do not really want me to come and talk about ministry and what it means to reach teens for Jesus Christ. Like Elaine, what they really want is for me to teach them how to do activities.

They want teens to come to a youth canoe trip, but they only see this as a fun social activity and not how it can be used to help the entire ministry develop and grow. My real work begins when I try to help the adult leadership team understand the difference between an activity-driven youth program and a model that uses activities to deepen the ministry to and with youth.

Simply stated, the activity-driven model is one designed to bring teens together for activities. There is really no goal beyond that, except the unspoken hope, which Elaine articulated, that by getting teens to attend activities, they might end up going to youth group and even worship services. There is the greater hope that with these fun activities, teens will learn to like going to church because they associate good times with church. So the theory is sort of like this: if we can get teens to come to our sponsored amusement park day, then they will see that church can be a fun place, and maybe they will give it a try.

Activities, though, are labor-intensive. They take a lot of time—if they are done well—to organize, promote, and implement. Success is usually determined by whether teens come to the event. If a good number make it to the activity, then the youth leader can give a favorable report on the numbers involved. When the numbers are up for an activity, everyone (youth team, pastor, church council, and so forth) can be happy that the teens are doing something good.

Church councils seem to love activity-driven models. When the youth pastor or youth team gives a report to the council that shows a full slate of activities designed for teens, the council is impressed with all that the teens are doing, and the report gives the impression that teens are active in church.

There is something strange about the church in how we perpetuate the idea that a successful youth program is a *busy* program. The more teens we can say have been involved in activities, the more the council is supportive, and, hopefully, the more funds it will provide for more activities. It is a vicious cycle, and it really gets to be counterproductive to the overall mission of youth ministry.

I have seen youth leaders get caught in the trap of becoming event planners, organizing one activity after another. There are youth leaders right now who could walk out of church and get a job on any cruise line or in any resort because of their experience in organizing and planning events. Some even wonder if being an activity director is the reason they entered youth ministry in the first place.

The problem is that these activity-driven youth leaders either get burned out from being the local activity director, or they begin to get a gnawing feeling that nothing of depth is taking place in the lives of the teens who attend. Not too long after this feeling starts, the youth leadership team realizes that the activity model may be successful in getting teens to do things, but it lacks spiritual substance.

One youth leader I consulted with had become frustrated because she had built quite an activity machine. Her group was doing things all the time. The youth program was busy, and parents were happy that their teens found activities to do at the church. Even the pastor was happy that the youth group finally seemed to be getting somewhere, and the pastor liked that the youth ministry was an asset that attracted new members with children and teens.

The youth leader's frustration centered on the fact that she wondered if God wanted the group to be so busy. She questioned whether all these activities were really doing anything worthwhile in the teens' lives. She wondered how they could get out of the trap of doing one activity after another. Unfortunately, this youth leader is not alone.

I have witnessed many such churches with "successful" youth programs that were actually successful activity-driven models, and not ministries focused on empowering teens in Jesus Christ. The problem is that even when church members or youth leaders realize that they are merely producing a successful activity model, they do not know how to break free of it. They find themselves trapped because the church, as we have said, tends to like this model. Parents like the good, wholesome activities provided for their teens, and the pastor likes it as a drawing point for parents with children and teens.

The youth leader caught in the trap of an activity-driven ministry could not change course and had to leave the church in order to get a new start with a new philosophy. It was good for her, but the church suffered when its youth ministry took a dive. Suddenly people found out how much work this model had been, and they just did not pick up the slack.

If a youth leader recognizes this problem emerging and the leadership team keeps feeling unfulfilled, then they will eventually see the need for something more. Unfortunately, they may be so locked in to being activity-driven that they do not know how to move to something more fulfilling.

Not only will youth leaders become unfulfilled, but they will also see how an activity-driven model breaks down as teens' lives become more complicated. Ask any youth leader or parent, and they will tell you how busy their teens are with school, sports, work, and band. Teens today are busy—perhaps more so than any other teen generation in history.

The activity-driven model is a problem because the only thing holding the teens to the church is the activity. When the activity offers nothing more than something to do, it is not a strong factor in staying connected to the church. As teens get older and busier, the church activity simply becomes one of a growing list of activities that they must choose from each week. Sometimes the church activity will be selected, and sometimes it will not. Is this really what we want to accomplish? Do we simply want to be another item on a teen's list of options?

If all we offer is activities, then that is exactly what happens. Teens are not really choosing between church and school, or church and sports, but between two activities competing for the same time slot. When the church becomes just one of a teen's many choices, the church will sometimes win in the priority listing, and sometimes it will lose.

In activity-driven models, the commitment level is low, and the benefit is minimal. Hear me clearly: a teen's choice not to attend an activity may or may not have anything to do with their or their parents' commitment to the church. It really has to do with the product being offered and whether this product is more appealing than the competitor's (school, sports, work, etc.).

Recently I was in a planning session with a group of teen leaders who were trying to figure out the next date they would meet. To my surprise, two teens pulled out their Palm Pilots to check their schedules, three took out datebooks, and one used her cell phone to call her mother about the family's schedule. These are busy teens!

The question we have to ask is whether teens today need more things to do. In most areas, *teens do not need more activities for the sake of having something to do*. With such busy teens, activity-driven models compete for their discretionary time. This competition can be brutal, especially when the youth program is defined by activities, and success is measured by attendance.

When we use activity-driven models, we are not really getting to the heart of ministry. We may think that because the church is sponsoring it, it must be ministry, right? Not necessarily. When the activity is just one in a string of events for the youth group, we are really not offering anything more than what they might get at the YMCA, Scouts, 4H, or any other teen-based group. Sometimes the events and activities work, and sometimes they don't. When they don't work, we are able to blame teens' schedules, lack of parental support, or anything other than the model.

Listen up, youth leaders. Teens' schedules and parents are not the problem. The problem is the activity-driven model.

The Ministry-to-and-with-Youth Model

Is our purpose for providing youth ministry simply to get teens to attend activities? Or is the purpose to help teens on the journey into a deeper understanding of discipleship and service to Christ? Obviously, it is the latter. This does not mean we do not have fun activities, and it certainly does not mean that we do not provide programs for our teens. It does mean, however, that in youth ministry, we never do an activity outside of our overall purpose and goal. In other words, any activity undertaken needs to be done in relationship to the overall strategy of being a mission outpost for Jesus Christ and a center of spiritual formation.

Herein lies the difference between a youth program centered on activities and a youth ministry focused on assisting, coaching, and guiding teens into a deeper understanding of the spiritual life. An activity-driven model feels good and looks good if teens are coming; however, a youth ministry will be truly successful only to the extent that the leadership team is intentionally working to deepen and build the spiritual lives of teenagers. It succeeds further as teens become spiritually empowered participants in the ministry strategy of the local congregation.

What makes the church different from other teen activities? What can the church offer teens that they cannot get anywhere else? What is the point of bringing teens together at church? We know that church cannot outdo the activities that youth experience in school and other community-based organizations, so what do we have that is relevant to teens' lives? What is our niche in this competitive marketplace for teens' attention, time, and energy?

Here it is: our niche is the spiritual life. The church can offer something that teens are willing to invest time in, and we have something that takes them from activities to self-exploration.

Using Activities in the Youth Ministry Model

In a youth ministry, activities are never an end unto themselves, but a means to an end. Time and resources are scarce, and the availability of adult involvement is sometimes limited.

It is important that activities become a tool of the ministry, rather than drive the ministry. In the previous pages, I never said that activities were bad or unproductive. I did say, however, that an activity-driven model will not produce the desired long-term goal of having a high-impact youth ministry.

An authentic youth ministry challenges teens to enter deeply into the spiritual life. It encourages teens to enter that life through the use of spiritual disciplines (prayer, Bible study, fasting, and so forth). It gives teens opportunities to put their faith into practice through acts of service and compassion.

We have youth ministry not simply because we like teens and want them to have a good church experience while growing up. We want these things to happen, but these are secondary objectives.

We have youth ministry so that we can help awaken the spiritual God-given potential that is within every life. We have youth ministry so that teens can become actualized in the fullest meaning of the word. When we view youth ministry in this way, we move beyond youth activity to a ministry that is so much more than just being another choice among the many in a teen's life.

Youth ministry becomes a vital part of teens' expressions of their hearts, their minds, and their souls as they enter into a ministry of self-discovery and service. When youth ministry is approached this way, teens want to develop their spiritual lives, just as they want to develop their physical bodies through exercise and their minds through study.

Doesn't this make our efforts a little more meaningful than just getting drivers to go to the skating rink? Yet how do we move away from being activity-driven to being centered in a ministry of faith formation?

We begin by having a church community that understands why it exists and what its purpose is in the world. It takes adults who are on the journey themselves, who are willing to invest their lives in teens, who are willing to be vulnerable, who are willing to seek answers with teens, who are willing to listen, who are willing to guide, and who are willing to go the distance with teens in their spiritual lives (more on this in Chapters Five and Six).

So why have activities at all? Great question! Activities are fun, they build memories, they help adults experience teens in different settings, and they help teens experience adults in different settings. They allow all of us to connect on a whole different level that cannot be reached by sitting in a class or in worship.

In my first year as a youth pastor, I learned an important lesson about activities. I wanted to prove to the youth council, the senior pastor, and probably even to myself that I had been called to this ministry.

So I was being a Bible scholar, maintaining detailed lessons, and putting some activities together, but I just could not break through to the senior high guys. They would not let me into their world, and I am sure I was trying a little too hard.

Well, one day I was shooting some baskets in the church parking lot before anyone had arrived for our youth group meeting. Soon a car drove up, and out popped two senior high guys whom I had not connected with. They said that they had seen me as they drove by and had decided to stop and shoot with me. Then another couple of guys came, and before too long, we had enough to play a little three-on-three. What a blast we had! We worked together, we got sweaty, and we even had a crowd watching us before we had to call it quits and get into the meeting. And that night, the senior high guys stayed for the youth program.

I had a good time, but it was more than just a pickup game; it was a breakthrough with these teenage guys. All of a sudden they saw me in a different light—as a normal guy, someone who could sweat profusely and gasp for air, and someone who got angry when he missed an easy lay up. They were able to razz me about my "slow" movement to the basketball, and challenges to play again came from that night on. Not only did we play more basketball, but these guys began to invite me to watch games with them at their high school, and they met me for lunch during the summer to talk about what was going on in their lives.

That impromptu activity taught me how something as simple as playing a game of basketball can provide a window into the lives of teens that a year of youth group meetings would never have done. From that point on, I was committed to providing a regular schedule of activities in order to provide adults and teens the opportunity to experience each other apart from the often static experience of a church meeting.

The key thing to remember in planning activities is that they are tools that help us reach our overall goal of providing a high-impact, effective ministry to and with youth. When we understand this goal, activities become a strategic thrust in our overall youth ministry plan. When our teen leaders understand this goal, they become great advocates for designing activities they know will attract teens their age, and they can get excited about inviting friends who may not go to church to attend. Teen leaders empowered to design their own activities, knowing the activities are part of a larger plan—how cool is that?

Think about it. Let's say your teen leaders organize a swim party at a water park. They plan it, promote it, and encourage other church teens to invite their friends.

The day comes, and they are actually pumped up about an activity they have planned. They invite their friends, knowing that they will not only have a great time, but this activity will also be part of a greater plan to reach their friends for Jesus Christ. When they bring their friends, they will introduce them to adult leaders, and the adult leaders will be sure to begin building friendships with these new teens.

Overall, the group will have a great day at the water park. The teen leaders will have been responsible for planning and implementing the activity, and the adults will have had the opportunity to continue to build relationships with teens they already know, as well as begin new relationships with teens they are meeting for the first time.

As far as the teens are concerned, when they are planning a canoe trip, skating party, sled-riding party, or a service project, they are coming to have fun, and we want them to have fun. At the same time, adults on the ministry team and key teen leaders realize that the activity is only part of the overall strategy of building relationships with all the members of the group. Therefore, it becomes imperative that adults in youth ministry be willing to get truly involved and participate in youth activities (that is, go down the hill on the sled, skate around the rink a few times, splash the other canoes while traveling down the river, and so forth). When we use an activity to build relationships with teens, we are providing something that is part of our overall youth ministry strategy.

The benefit of this strategy is that teens will realize that they are with adults who genuinely like being with them and who like to have fun. As this develops, you will find that teens are choosing to come to an activity not just because it is the best choice on a particular day or night, but because they want to be with people who like being with them and believe they have something to offer. An activity is not successful in terms of how many teens come, but rather in terms of the relationships developed or strengthened during the activity.

Refocus on the Purpose of Ministry with Youth

Your adult members will be far more inspired by this ministry because it is not about just giving teens something to do. It takes youth ministry to a whole new level, where strategy and planning are all about moving teens to a deeper reality of who they are as children of God and disciples of Jesus Christ. It is truly about helping them enter a place of empowerment that is unlike anything they could have imagined. Any activity we do needs to be part of a much larger strategy of creating an atmosphere where teens (and adults) are awakening to the spiritual life. Bet you didn't think that a trip to the movies and pizza afterwards could create so much cosmic significance, did you? It really can!

So let's turn the corner and get refocused on the purpose and place of activities in youth ministry. Activities are great when they are designed in the context of an overall ministry of reaching teens for Christ. As your team of adults and teen leaders gathers to plan activities, encourage them to keep the larger picture in mind. Ask them how this or that event or activity will assist them in moving toward the larger goal of guiding teens deeper into discipleship.

Of course, adults who are involved in the youth ministry need to buy into this model. The adults need to be willing to build relationships with teens, to invest their lives in teens, and to discuss faith issues. Your team should never do an activity just for the sake of doing an activity—it is too easy to get caught in the trap of becoming a church activity director. Everything needs to support the primary purpose of the ministry. Keep that focus, and the activities will be a source of strength and empowerment for your overall ministry.

Key Points

- Activities are never an end in themselves; such activities will always be defined as successful only with regard to the number in attendance.
- Activity-driven models take a great deal of time and energy to organize, market, and implement.
- Activity-driven models need to maintain a high level of excitement in order to compete with all the other choices teens have.
- Activity-driven models usually end up being one of many choices older teens have on a long list of competing events and activities.
- Activities are a good *tool* for creating an atmosphere where relationships can develop between teens and adults, as well as among the teens themselves.
- Activities are great when adults realize that they are opportunities to get to know teens in a nonthreatening environment.
- Activities are great when they become part of the overall strategy of reaching teens for Jesus Christ.
- Breaking out of the activity-driven model is difficult, but it can be done.

Now What?

1. Do you have an activity-driven program or a youth ministry? How many activities have you done in the past six months?

_____

_____

What were the goals of these activities? Were they reached?

_____

_____

_____

_____

2. How are teens employed to help assist the adults in developing activities that are meaningful to and exciting for teens in the church and community?

_____

_____

_____

_____

3. Evaluate each activity. Is it seen as an outreach opportunity, or is it just something fun to do?

_____

_____

_____

_____

_____

4. What follow-up exists for unchurched teens who attend an activity sponsored by your youth ministry?

_____

_____

_____

_____

_____

5. If you are a youth leader/director/volunteer stuck in an activity-driven model, list some ways you can begin to use the activities to support your mission of creating disciples.

_____

_____

_____

_____

_____

Chapter Five
Principle #4

A healthy youth ministry intentionally recruits a diverse team of spiritually open and spiritually developing adult leaders.

G abrielle couldn't wait for the first day of junior high. She began learning to play the flute during the summer in hopes of getting into the school band. With her summer instructor's help, she carefully prepared a piece of music to play at her audition. The audition went well, and even though her performance was a little shaky, the team of students holding the audition thought she would develop well and accepted her into their stage band.

The first day of band finally arrived, and Gabi couldn't wait. Would this be everything she had thought? She took a seat with the other students and prepared her instrument. Suddenly, the door opened and the new band instructor walked in, introduced himself, and said, "Hello, class. You all look ready to play, but you know what? I have to be honest and tell you that I really haven't played my own instrument since I was in junior high. I figure I can learn it again, and together we will learn some music to play at our first assembly in two weeks."

Gabi and the whole class were shocked into silence by what they had just heard.

Experience Counts!

Granted, this is a silly illustration, but it makes a point. Does the band instructor qualify to be the bandleader just because he once played a musical instrument? Of course not! Students like Gabi had prepared and developed their skills for the band experience, only to have a leader who could not help them be better as a band than any one of them could be as an individual.

Parents too expect that a bandleader not only be proficient in a musical instrument, but know how to read music, draw a band together, and select music based on the band's ability. The same could be said for sports coaches, driving instructors, scout leaders, and just about anyone responsible for teaching a teen a skill or activity. If we can agree that this is true—that parents expect competence from their teens' teachers—then why does this truth not intersect with church life? Church seems to be the only place where parents send their children for instruction without ever wondering, checking, or observing the instructors' abilities or skills.

Think about that for a minute. I have two children, and over the years we have taken them to lessons in swimming, gymnastics, music, drama, weightlifting, karate, basketball, and many other activities. Before we ever take them to a lesson, we know who is sponsoring it (the YMCA, the school, private instructors, and so forth). We also find out who will actually be teaching the class. When we find out, we ask the instructors what they plan to do, what they hope to accomplish, and what our children should have learned by the end of the class.

In many cases, instructors hold orientations for parents to let them know these very things. They are up front with what they hope to accomplish and what they hope the students will have learned by the end of the class. This helps parents feel confident about our knowledge of what they are doing, and it allows us to feel as if we are leaving our children in capable hands.

In all these years, we have never met a coach, teacher, or instructor who was unwilling to sit and talk to us about their philosophy, their background, and their goals for the class. My wife and I are not unusual in this way. We know that many other parents do the same kind of research. So what happens when we get to church? Why is it different there?

When we are building a youth ministry, we need to have more than just caring adults, adults who have certain talents, charismatic individuals, or even those who do it because no one else will. All these are admirable attributes, but they mean little if our adult leaders are not on spiritual journeys themselves. Like the bandleader in the example, we often have wonderful people who went to youth group when they were teens, but they have not been intentional about their spiritual journeys for years. Unless our adult guides and mentors are intentionally on that journey, our church will never have the long-term impact that we all hope for in the lives of our teens.

I doubt that parents will all of a sudden be checking out the spiritual resumes of youth leaders and Sunday school teachers to ensure they know what they are doing. So it becomes critical that the youth leadership team and the staff of the church hold one another in loving accountability for personal faith formation.

One church I worked with had a youth leader everyone loved. The teens thought he was great. He had a good family, his wife was involved (some of the teens even called her Mom), and he developed a working ministry with the teens. He even knew that the teens should be getting connected to Christ, and he wanted to see that happen.

In spite of this, something was lacking in the youth group. We began to look at his own spiritual discipline. He was unique in that he was able to get real with me quickly. He told me up front that he only read the Bible when preparing a lesson, and his praying amounted to dinner and bedtime prayers with his children. I think he got so real so quickly because he knew I was not there to judge him. He wanted to take the teens to the next level, and he was tired of being an activity director.

In addition, his church did not offer any adult classes outside of Sunday morning, and the pastor did not emphasize a spiritual journey with the staff. The staff rarely prayed in a way that went beyond concerns voiced at staff meetings. The congregation did not have a strategic plan to reach people for Jesus Christ, and it did not have any kind of spiritual accountability for how members were personally growing in Christ. Basically, the church had a nice staff, serving a nice church, doing a nice ministry that was getting by with nice people. Thankfully, this youth pastor knew that something more needed to happen in his own life.

After our time together, we began to see that there would be no significant spiritual breakthrough in the teens' lives, in the youth group, or in the entire church until there was a spiritual breakthrough in his own life. (I was hoping for a breakthrough with the pastor and other staff as well, but they had not asked me to consult with them.) So, wanting to ensure that his breakthrough happened, he knew he had to get intentional about his spiritual journey, regardless of what was happening at church.

He discovered that a church in a nearby community was offering a midweek Bible study, so he began attending. He formed a prayer group with other adult youth leaders in the community, and a few of those leaders agreed to meet weekly for accountability checks to see how they were doing with individual prayer and Bible study. The more he took seriously his spiritual life, the more he began to realize that there was a transformation taking place in the spirituality of the youth group. All his charisma and abilities were greatly enhanced as he reached out and added the spiritual dimension that had previously been lacking in his youth ministry.

I have met incredibly wonderful adults working in youth ministry who are still struggling with their own faith development. I have met adults who love teens, but they are not so sure about their love of God. I have met adults who have an incredible ability to organize youth activities but cannot seem to organize their own lives.

Does this mean they are bad people? Not at all! Am I saying you have to be perfect to be an adult in youth ministry? Of course not. What I am saying is that adults in youth ministry need to be on a spiritual journey. They need to be involved in a process that helps them develop as disciples of Jesus Christ. They need to be seeking continued ways of developing that spiritual life. Is this asking too much? No way! If we are going to be responsible about our ministry to and with youth, then we need to have adults who are actively pursuing the spiritual life in ways that demonstrate a growing understanding of who they are in Christ.

This book does not have the space to discuss in totality the issues presented here, so allow me to get right to the point. The bottom line is that it is easy to coast along spiritually in mainline churches across America. Seldom is anyone encouraged to share where they are spiritually, right? When was the last time anyone in church really spoke to you about how your heart was doing in Christ?

We tend to sit in the same place in church next to the same people Sunday after Sunday, year after year, and we rarely, if ever, talk about issues of the heart. Literally, a person can be active in a mainline church, be caring, be good, be compassionate, be involved in the yearly church bazaar, and no one would ever question whether that person had made a commitment to follow the spiritual life. We just assume that if people are in church, then they have some level of connection. This is not a safe assumption.

People come to church seeking many different things. Instead of helping them find what they are seeking, we often simply work hard to get them involved in church. It is almost as if the busier we can make church people, the more we can help them feel like they really are where God wants them to be. (This can also explain why so many youth ministries are busy doing activities.)

This leads us right back to the beginning of the book when we looked at how the overall church ministry impacts the youth ministry. If our adults are not being actively challenged to pursue Christ with all their hearts, souls, and minds, how can we expect them to provide a ministry that encourages teens to seek Christ with all their hearts, souls, and minds? Yet if we are going to have a high-impact, long-term youth ministry, it can only be done to the extent that we have adults willing to invest their lives in the lives of teens. Not only that, but we also want adults who are intentionally on a spiritual journey.

What Can You Do Now?

So where are we going to find these adults? I mean, most churches are happy just to have adults take some responsibility for the youth program by leading a few activities. So where do we start?

First, take a fearless inventory of your own spiritual life. Do you read your Bible? How often? How about prayer? Do you have friends with whom you speak about spiritual issues on a regular basis? In what ways have you spiritually matured since this time last year? Do you have a spiritual mentor who provides a listening ear, who asks probing questions, and who offers words of wisdom about your spiritual journey?

These are just some questions to get you thinking, but hopefully you can see where this is headed. You may be reading this and thinking, "Whoa! I am not where I need to be, and I don't know how to get there!" If this is true, please be patient with yourself. It is like looking in the mirror and seeing those extra pounds that have to go. They won't go overnight—it takes time. Be patient, but do not wait for next week before you begin.

Here are some things you can do right now: join a prayer group, get into a Bible study, take a spiritual retreat, or form an accountability circle with friends. You can also ask your pastor (or another mature spiritual leader) to mentor you. Set up a schedule to meet on a regular basis for the purpose of helping you move more deeply into your spiritual life.

Through this intentional attention to spiritual things, you will open your heart to God in a way you never dreamed possible. You will deepen your own spiritual life, and in doing so, you will begin to develop a sensitivity that helps you discern how the Spirit is moving in the lives of the adults on your team and the teens involved in the ministry.

Where Can We Find New Leaders?

How do we recruit new adults for the team? Where do we find them? These are two important questions, because how we answer them will affect the ministry of your church. So let's take them one at a time.

Our local youth basketball league is a feeder program for the high school program. Beginning in fourth grade, girls and boys in our town begin to learn the style of play that is coached at the junior- and senior-high levels. The philosophy is that if they learn the style and team concepts at this age, when they get to junior and senior high, they will not have to spend a great deal of time on the basics. Instead, they can concentrate on offensive and defensive strategies based on a system they already know.

When looking for adults to be involved in the ministry to and with youth, look to the feeder programs in your church. Feeder programs are any programs, activities, or experiences that help adults deepen their spiritual lives. These programs encourage adults to own the primary mission of the congregation. In these programs we will find many adults who will be involved in the active ministry of guiding youth to the spiritual life.

First, look at what is going on in your church. Which adults do you notice involved in Bible studies other than the ones offered in Sunday school? Is there a men's group that focuses on the spiritual life? Does your church sponsor a moms' support group? Are there adults who take spiritual retreats? What other activities go on in your church?

Wherever people take the time to nurture their spiritual lives with these kinds of activities, you will find people who have a desire, a call, and an inward leaning to go deeper into the heart of God. It is from this pool that you will find leaders who will be effective in reaching out to the teens in your church. These groups hold your future mentors and guides.

Personally, I do not care if these adults are young, middle-aged, or seniors. If they have a passion for God, if they are actively pursuing the spiritual life, and if they are open to sharing it with others, then they have the potential to serve in ministry to and with youth.

Who Should We Recruit?

Ideally, our team will consist of adults who vary in age, marital status, and education levels. We need senior adults who are willing to invest in teenagers' lives as much as we need young adults. We need married couples who are willing to work together as much as single adults, and we benefit from having people who are musically inclined, as well as those who love sports. The more diversity we are able to establish on our team, the more opportunity we will have for reaching a wide range of teens in our church and community.

The critical factor for all the adults is that they continue their spiritual development after accepting the call to be on the ministry team. It is best if they can continue developing together. In order for this to happen, one of the requirements for serving on the youth ministry team may be a willingness to meet regularly as a small group. You may agree to meet on a weekly basis for the purpose of prayer, Bible study, and reflection on the course and focus of your youth ministry.

When adult leaders work on their spiritual lives together, they set a huge example for the youth about mentoring relationships. They also show that they do not have it all together and that they continue to need a small-group experience to support and encourage their own spiritual formation.

Can anyone say *authenticity*? Talking about the spiritual life is good, but when our actions match our words, we are able to show that, regardless of our age, we will always need each other and the community of faith to walk this journey.

When teens see that their adult leaders also have mentors and spiritual friends that they meet with, they will realize that adults are not perfect and that they are still working out their own journeys. By meeting in small spiritual-formation groups, the adults also begin to blow away the whole activity-driven model. In fact, what happens is the adult leaders begin to experience a profound shift in how they relate to teens, to each other, and to the ministry in general. These weekly meetings move beyond simply planning programs and activities; they become places where the adults are truly seeking what God is doing in the lives of the students and in the overall ministry.

I have a friend who is a high school football coach. Every week during football season, the entire coaching staff gets together to review the previous week's game, evaluate players, and begin putting together a game plan for next week. These meetings are imperative to the success of the team's overall mission of winning games. When the team loses, these meetings can be difficult, because the coaches have to look at themselves to see how they may have contributed to the loss. Walking out of these meetings, the coaches have a game plan and words of encouragement for the players, and they know what needs to be done during the week to prepare for the next game.

Our leadership meetings will accomplish much the same kinds of things as my friend's coaches meetings. We will be able to review what took place the week before, talk about teens and where they are spiritually, pray for the teens, suggest ways to encourage the teens, and begin to lay the groundwork for the coming week. These meetings will help the team focus, grow, and develop a strong sense of cohesion.

When we move in this direction, we do not have to find adults who have it all together (as if that were possible). We simply need to find adults who love God and are willing to be on the journey with others.

You are also going to meet adults who want to be involved but are scared and feel inadequate because of what they do not know. Listen. If an adult loves God and loves teens, then we can work with those attributes. If adults feel inadequate because they know they have not been intentional in their spiritual lives, we can work with that! The adult just needs to be willing to enter a process of spiritual formation that may include: 1) meeting with a spiritual mentor (preferably the pastor or another trusted individual) on a short-term basis to discuss his or her journey; 2) taking a Bible study class to become familiar with the Scriptures; 3) keeping a prayer journal; and 4) being involved in an accountability group. Any of these, or any combination, can give the adult the confidence to walk with teens on their spiritual journeys.

Three years ago, I began to assist in coaching my son's youth football team. It had been a *lot* of years since I played football. In that first year of coaching I discovered that even though I had played, and even though I have watched football all these years, I was not qualified to coach football to a group of children learning for the first time.

Thankfully, there were some dads who had been coaching for several years. I began to watch them, ask them questions, and take a little bit of responsibility here and there as I became reacquainted with the technical aspects of the game. During the intervening year, I got serious about learning how to coach football. I read about it, listened to former coaches, and watched coaching videos. Even though I still have more to learn about football and coaching, I am more prepared now, going into my fourth year, than I was in that first year. I now feel confident that I can help another dad whose skills are somewhat rusty become a coach for today's young players.

In the same way, we can mentor and walk with adults who do not feel that they are spiritual enough or together enough for youth ministry. Soon these adults will see that none of us is that together, and we need one another to stay faithful to what God has called us to do. There is something liberating when we have teammates who know us and who realize the struggles we face, yet are still willing to be our friends and walk with us on the journey. The skills we learn from relating to other adults are the skills that will create a high-impact youth ministry that goes the distance.

What About Our Current Leaders?

The question that comes up right about now is, "I like this new concept, but what about the other adults who are currently on the team? What if they do not want to get focused in this way?"

Here's the deal: if our purpose has been to plan activities, and this whole spiritual thing is something that we have not focused on, then we will need to talk to our team about making the shift. Believe it or not, there will be some in your group who will be so thankful for the change that they will jump on board immediately. They are the ones who get drained by all the activities. They leave each week wondering why they do it and thinking how they cannot wait for their children to graduate so they do not have to do it anymore.

By moving in this new direction, you will give them purpose. They will see value in what they are called to, and they will find themselves becoming enriched and spiritually charged by this new direction. On the other hand, you may have others who, for a number of reasons, will not feel comfortable as you make these changes.

The thing that the leader needs to do is be clear on why the changes are being made and why the bar is being raised. Talk about your heart's desire for the teens in your group: that they truly learn how to empower their lives through a relationship with Jesus Christ. Affirm your belief that God has a plan for these teens and a plan for the leadership team. In order to realize these plans, it becomes necessary for the team members to intentionally walk their journey of faith together. Talk about the need to read the Scriptures, to pray, and to seek God's guidance as they seek to guide the teens, as well as the importance of knowing how to assist teens in their spiritual journeys. Lay out what that means for you as the leader and for the entire team. (In Chapter Six, we will talk about what it means to have an intentional process of discipleship for teens.)

Let the team know that you understand this is a new expectation, and there is no shame if someone wants to step aside, as this will be different from what they signed up to do. Yet encourage the adults to stick with it. If they enter this journey with you, they will realize a youth ministry they never dared think was possible.

Some adults may decide to leave, but most will stay. This new adult team will now be on a journey toward establishing a high-impact, long-term youth ministry that will give teens the skills to be disciples of Jesus Christ.

The primary spiritual mentor for the adult team will be the youth leader. The youth leader's strength will be in how he or she is able to mentor and disciple these adults so that they in turn can mentor and disciple teens. Yes, this means that the primary ministry group for the youth leader is *not* the youth, but the adults who are actively mentoring and developing relationships with the teens.

When this takes place, the church benefits in a powerful way. When the youth leader leaves (and they do leave), the ministry will not have to suffer as it waits for someone new to take over. Just because the youth leader leaves does not mean that the youth ministry will fail. The ministry will continue as the search process gets underway. The strength of the youth ministry will be in the way the youth leader is able to invest in the lives of the adults serving on the team.

Does this mean that the youth leader does not connect with the youth? No, not at all. It simply means the youth leader does not attempt to invest in all the youth. That is what the other adults are there to do. The youth leader will still have a group of teens (usually the ones who are emerging as key leaders) in whom he or she invests time to help them develop into effective spiritual leaders. The rest of the teens will be cared for by the adults serving in the ministry.

What About Parents As Youth Leaders?

I wish I had a dime for every time I've been asked that question. There are all kinds of philosophies on parents in youth ministry. Too many people automatically assume that teens do not want their parents involved. This can be an incorrect assumption.

Here's my rule of thumb: before asking a parent to participate in youth ministry, ask that parent's teen if it would be okay to invite the parent. By asking teens, we show respect for their feelings and enable them to be part of the process.

If the teen says he or she would not feel comfortable with the parent involved, respect that response, and do not approach the parent. In my experience, teens more often say yes than no.

Inviting Adults to Participate in Youth Ministry

When you identify adults who may be a good fit for youth ministry, here is a simple plan for inviting them to participate:

(1) Provide the name(s) of the adult(s) you are considering to the teen leaders. If there is a consensus that this person may be a good match, go on to Step 2. If the teens do not think this is a good match right now, honor that.

(2) Invite the adult(s) to act as chaperone(s) at a one-time event (i.e., a car wash, a concert, or a ball game). A one-time event will prevent the adults from feeling as if they have committed to anything long-term. At the same time, if things do not work out, the youth group will not be obligated to stay with someone who is not a good match.

(3) During the event, observe how the adults interact with the teens. If they relate well, go on to Step 4. If they do not connect, then thank them for chaperoning, and tell them you may call on them again.

(4) Ask the adults who connect to the teens to attend a few other activities to continue the relationship-building. Other adults on the youth ministry team should ensure that the new adult is engaging the teens on a personal level. Following the third or fourth event, the youth leader should talk to the adults to see how they feel about these events.

(5) Teen leaders meet again to discuss their feelings about the new adult "chaperones" and whether they are connecting. If everyone is in agreement, go on to Step 6.

(6) Members of the teen council (the teens themselves) invite the adults to be part of the youth ministry team.

(7) At the next meeting, the adults are introduced to the entire group as new members of the youth ministry team (at which time there is wild applause).

This process gives the teens ownership. It does not commit anyone to a long-term involvement, and it allows youth and adults to get a feel for whether God is bringing this together.

Diversity Is Essential

It is critical that the leader encourage diversity on the team. People are going to be at different places in their spiritual journeys. They are going to have different ideas about how God relates to us. As we are developing the team, it is essential to allow people to express what they are experiencing or what they believe in a safe, nonjudgmental environment. This does not mean that everyone has to agree (this isn't heaven), but it does mean that we need to foster an attitude of respect for where people are on the team.

The only requirement is that we need to be in agreement about where we are going and what we hope to accomplish as a team. I believe that God builds a diverse group of team members so that we can expand our outreach to all those subculture groups that make up the world of the teenager. We need adult introverts as much as we need extroverts, athletes as much artists, single adults as much as married adults, and young adults as much as older adults. As our teens witness a diverse team working together, they will get a strong image of how the church reaches a diverse world.

Now What?

1. How are adults currently recruited for the youth team in your congregation?

_____

_____

_____

_____

2. What requirements or expectations are there for the adult team members who work with youth in your congregation?

_____

_____

_____

_____

3. Are people—both youth leaders and others—aware of these expectations?

_____

4. In what ways are adults mentored by the church staff?

_____

_____

_____

_____

_____

5. In what ways are adults encouraged to continue an intentional approach to faith formation?

_____

_____

_____

_____

_____

Chapter Six
Principle #5

*A healthy youth ministry has an intentional
process for teen spiritual formation.*

I f there is one constant in the lives of teens, it is that every day they
interact with adults other than their parents. They interact with school
teachers, music teachers, dance instructors, coaches, driver's ed
instructors, managers at part-time jobs, and scout leaders. All of these
adults share a similar goal and responsibility: to help teens develop some
aspect of their bodies, minds, and/or spirits.

So, when teens go to choir practice, they expect the choir director to
teach them how to sing a piece of music. When teens go to driver's ed,
they expect the instructor to teach them how to drive. When teens go to
softball practice, they expect the coach to teach them how to improve
batting and fielding. When teens go camping with a scout troop, they
expect the scout leader to teach them everything from pitching a tent to
cooking over an open fire.

OK, I think I have made my point, but in case I have left any doubt,
here it is: teens are more than used to the idea of having adults as
instructors/teachers/guides/coaches. In nearly every aspect of teens'
lives, there is someone, usually an adult, to provide instruction. In order
for the student to become proficient, the adult needs to be proficient in
what he or she is teaching. Makes sense, doesn't it?

What applies to the everyday world of teenagers outside of church
can apply to their church experiences as well. The entire purpose of
investing in the lives of teens is to build relationships that will help them
experience and develop their spiritual lives. Adults are crucial to this

process. They cannot give up their responsibility to guide the next generation to a vital and authentic spiritual life.

An Intentional Approach to Spiritual Formation

Teens encounter guides intent on helping them reach goals in just about every area of their lives except spiritual formation. It seems as if mainline churches have had a brain lapse when it comes to knowing how, or seeing the need for, assisting people in developing intentional strategies for faith formation. The things that work in the real world—training skills, athletic development, and proficiency tests—are not applied in church.

A piano teacher knows that a student will not learn how to play simply by listening to a pianist play. A volleyball coach knows that players will not develop skills and strategies simply by watching a game. Yet the unspoken strategy in many churches is that teens will someone how connect to their spiritual lives simply by sitting in worship.

Why is there such a disconnection when it comes to developing faith formation? When we look at the problem from this perspective, it is easy to see why teens (and probably most adults) say that church is boring and irrelevant.

For all practical purposes, the typical church has few expectations for faith formation. The main expectation is that people attend. Thus, the primary goal of many churches is simply to exist. The church establishes a low level of expectations that teens and adults gladly meet. The focus for youth ministry is not on faith formation, but on keeping the teens coming to church.

This may sound harsh, but we have to be honest if we are going to break the mold. There may be an underlying hope that our teens will develop as faithful disciples of Jesus Christ, but until that hope becomes an intentional ministry, it may be seldom fulfilled.

Too often the church falls into this trap of low expectations, where people are not challenged to intentionally develop their spiritual lives. You may be thinking, "Now wait a minute! We offer Sunday school, worship, youth group, and even a midweek prayer service." If you do, great; you are doing all the things that a church is expected to do. Unless there is individual contact with members, though, most of these spiritual activities are hit-or-miss. It is like shooting an arrow at a target with your eyes closed.

This approach to church does not just apply to youth; it is what most adults have grown to expect. They have been living with such low expectations for faith formation that they simply perpetuate the idea that the purpose of going to church is to keep church going. How did we ever take the awesome experience of God filling our lives and boil it all down to just needing to go to church?

If you are wondering whether your church has low expectations, consider these questions:

- Does your church have membership vows for people who join? If so, are they held accountable to those vows?
- Does your church use any sort of criteria for recruiting Sunday school teachers?
- When people come to worship, do they expect to encounter Christ in a way that affects their lives and experiences?
- Can you remember the last time anyone in church asked you about your spiritual life?

If you answered no to any or all of these questions, then you have just unveiled the primary reason we have so little spiritual-formation instruction for teens: when our adults have had little in the way of intentional spiritual formation and have lived with low expectations, they may feel as though they have little to give to teens. The point is that if our teens are not being challenged to go deeper spiritually, then it is truly symptomatic of issues the entire church is facing.

Let's review this chapter's opening assertion: teens live most of their days surrounded by adult instructors, coaches, and guides. The church is called to be part of the holistic development of each person's life. It is responsible for assisting all people in spiritual formation. The church needs to and can be the center of teen spirituality, where teens can explore, in a loving and caring environment, the depths of who they are as spiritual beings. In this environment, they can share their questions, their doubts, and their insights with adults who are willing to see them as individuals and to walk with them as they struggle to discover who they are as children of God.

How can we create this environment? How can we create a place that provides instruction, guidance, and hope? How can we create a place where teens feel free to talk about their successes and failures? How can we raise expectations without being oppressive?

First, meet with your pastor to discuss the development of an intentional process for spiritual formation among adults in the congregation. How can you include such practices as loving accountability for membership vows and hiring spiritually qualified Sunday school teachers? What other things can you do to raise the expectations for adult spiritual formation?

Once you have met with your pastor and determined a course of action for the adults, the youth leadership team, including key teen leaders, can explore the process for teen spiritual formation. Begin by mapping out every area of the church where there is an opportunity to be involved in the lives of teens. Most churches have Sunday school (which we will talk about in depth in pages to follow), youth group, and worship. In addition, there may be a youth choir, a sports ministry, a scouting ministry, midweek Bible studies, community service projects, and even teen prayer groups. In all these areas, adults can connect to teens and offer guidance, encouragement, and inspiration.

It is essential that the youth leadership team stake a claim in all these areas. I have seen too many churches where there is no connection between the youth group and the Sunday school, or no connection between the youth ministry and the music or sports ministries. It is counterproductive not to bring all these areas together in an attempt to develop an intentional approach to spiritual formation for teens.

After the team diagrams every area where teens connect to the church, we then seek to implement a strategy that includes all these areas. The team must be able to meet a diverse group of teens where they are physically and accept them for where they are spiritually. (We'll talk about that in a moment.) In a perfect setting, there are enough adults to work all these different areas. For example, the youth ministry team can be subdivided into the youth group team, the youth choir team, the youth sports team, the youth Sunday school class team, and so forth, and the adults can choose the degree to which they want to be involved.

Unfortunately, few of us live in a perfect situation. Initially, your team may need to focus on those areas with the greatest potential for adult-teen interaction, with the goal of eventually covering all the areas in your church that affect the lives of teens. The key thing team members need to remember is that, more than being involved in a class or ministry, the adults' number one priority is to build relationships with teens.

Do not ever forget this basis for youth ministry: people develop their spiritual lives through relationships, not creative programs. Programs draw teens together, but it is the quality of adult-teen relationships that helps them enter more deeply into the spiritual life.

In their book *The God-Bearing Life*, Dean and Foster describe this relational process in a way that is helpful and appropriate for ministry to and with teens. Too often youth ministry teams focus on running the program, rather than on taking the time to build relationships. The old adage is true—people don't care how much you know until they know how much you care. Teens will be involved in spiritual formation when they know that the adults truly care about them. This is what is meant by ministry to and *with* youth.

So far, we have said that the youth ministry team needs to:
- critically examine the existing process for adult spiritual formation;
- determine where teens are connecting with the church;
- decide how to deploy the youth team to those areas;
- build relationships with teens. This is the number one priority.

Since we have developed a picture of our youth ministry that is beyond the Sunday night youth group, what do we do now? The next step is to develop a process by which you move teens into a deeper understanding of who they are as disciples of Jesus Christ.

One of the very best books I have ever read on this topic is *Purpose-Driven Youth Ministry*, by Doug Fields. In his book, Fields gives a clear process of teen spiritual development to which I do not believe I can add anything further. He lays out a plan by which teens enter the church and develop as disciples of Jesus Christ.

My only comment about Fields' process is that you will need to adapt it to your particular situation. The book is based on the assumption that you already have a strong adult ministry from which to draw disciples. This may not be true for your church, so you may need to modify the process while you and your team are raising expectations for adult spiritual formation.

We are moving now! We have identified the areas of youth ministry and determined how we are going to cover those areas. We are focused on relational evangelism, and we have determined a process to move teens deeper spiritually. Now we just have to get them into the process.

Getting Focused on One Area of Spiritual Formation

In this section, I am not laying out an entire process for spiritual formation. Instead, I want to take the most overlooked and underrated area of youth ministry and build a plan for using this area as a focal point for teen spiritual formation. Can you guess which area that might be? If you answered Sunday school, you get the gold star! Why focus on Sunday school? Because for many of our teens, Sunday school is the primary gateway to spiritual formation.

Most families in today's culture give one and maybe even two hours a week on Sunday morning for church and spiritual formation. Not only that, but it can be easier for us to recruit adults to serve as mentors and spiritual friends during this time. Adults are more willing (initially anyway) to serve during the time when they are already committed to being in church.

Adults live incredibly busy lives, especially if they have children. Trying to get a commitment beyond Sunday morning is difficult. Please lose the idea that adults would commit if they were really dedicated to the church; that simply is not true. Many adults are trying their best, in the midst of hectic schedules, to attend to their families' spiritual development. Sunday morning is a great time to get your developing, maturing adults to commit to opening relationships with teens.

Our Sunday morning spiritual-formation opportunities are so overlooked that in some churches, youth staff and adult youth leaders defer to the Sunday school department, which works separately from the overall youth ministry strategy. To let this incredible opportunity slip by makes no sense. A church is more likely to have a diverse group of teens in Sunday morning worship than in the weekly youth program.

I have spoken to youth leaders from small and large churches alike who have no idea what takes place in youth Sunday school, and they have no real connection with the Sunday school teachers. Even if there is a connection, there is no intentional process that combines the strategies of the youth ministry with those of the Sunday school program.

A New Vision for Sunday Morning Spiritual Formation

We need to realize that building a center of spiritual formation on a school model is not going to cut it. For years we have placed our children and teens in grade-related Sunday school classes, regardless of their spiritual development. Sorry for being so blunt, but this is just stupid.

Think about it. Just about everything we study has a starting point, as well as a way to measure progress and move us to the next level. So a grade-related model makes little sense in an active process for spiritual formation. This model lowers students' expectations, because the teacher is forced to give elementary lessons to a class in which some of the teens may be more spirituality advanced than others.

Karate, on the other hand, is an excellent teaching model. This sport has an entry point for everyone. Regardless of whether you are five years old or fifty-five, you will start at the same place, learn the same skills, and be challenged by the same skill assessment. Adult beginners will most likely be in a separate class from children beginners, but they will be learning the same skills. The adult beginners *may* advance faster than the children, but they still have to go through the same training and assessment tests, regardless of how old they are or how good their physical conditioning is upon entry. For many years, karate has demonstrated the importance of all people beginning the journey at the same place, while progressing at one's own pace.

Yet in regard to spiritual instruction, we treat everyone the same. This makes no sense. It makes me wonder what the point of Sunday school is. If the point is simply to provide a nice lesson that has no real value, impact, or relation to the real world, then it does not really matter what we do, does it? Our best hope is that children and teens will get something by osmosis. Have we ever stopped to consider that osmosis does not work for learning math? Why do we think it will work for spiritual formation?

The majority of children and teens will put up with this method because they have to, but they will enter adulthood having learned little about being disciples of Jesus Christ in the real world. Because of this, I am convinced that the majority of Sunday school programs are practically worthless, simply because so few people are learning anything.

The youth team needs to recapture the creativity and power of the morning hours and develop them into opportunities to take teens deeper into the heart of God. Our primary objective for Sunday mornings is to guide teens into spiritual formation through Bible study, service, and interactive lessons.

When churches do not have any systematic approach to spiritual formation, Sunday school superintendents and staff are often depressed because they cannot retain teachers, and teacher recruitment has become one of *the* most dreaded experiences that a Sunday school committee faces each year. Too often, Sunday school is simply a place where a creative, rather than spiritual, experience is desired. So is it any wonder that our Sunday school classes continue to decline in attendance?

The decline is not about people not caring or not trying hard enough. I want to make that clear, because I know Sunday school teams that work extremely hard but still get minimal results. In my opinion, the decline is due to a whole generation of children growing up in irrelevant, boring Sunday schools and now, as adults, making a conscious decision that they will not inflict the same experience on their children.

Currently, my children attend a Sunday school that uses the rotation model. In theory, this is one of the most exciting advancements in Sunday school ministry in the past decade. It is also labor-intensive. We celebrate the fact that this model depends heavily on a relational approach, but if the relational aspect is not developed, the rotation model becomes a new approach that is helpful simply because it is new.

In our church, the relational piece is missing. The best thing I can say about it is that my children prefer it to what was used in previous years. They like it because it has variety, they enjoy the classes, and they have some idea of what to expect.

So are they learning anything? Has the program helped them to move further along their spiritual journeys than they were a year ago? Not particularly, but then again, how would we know? There are no benchmarks along the way, and there is no skill assessment. They do have a pleasant experience that is building good feelings about going to church. Believe me, I am thankful for that, because it is at least something.

When Sunday schools shift to this kind of model, they are correctly judging that the traditional model is not working. Yet these interactive models will only be effective when they are seen as part of an intentional strategy to move people along the path of discipleship. If we try new models as a way to get people interested, then they will have limited success. If, however, we can utilize the very best of what they represent, then we will be building a strong foundation for spiritual formation.

Likewise, using grade-related models to pursue spiritual goals is ineffective. So rather than herding people into predetermined groups, we must assess what they need to take their next steps in faith. We must design a process that helps each individual progress at a comfortable yet challenging pace that moves them forward in spiritual development.

In order to become effective centers of spiritual formation, we need to be merciless in our evaluation of our current educational models. We need to set up a progressive model of instruction that is centered on the church mission and vision and grounded in the church's core values. If our core value is to make and mature disciples of Jesus Christ, then how is our system of spiritual formation supporting this? How can it be measured? How do we know we are making progress? What are our benchmarks for faith development?

Ouch! There is the problem. Can we measure progress? Absolutely! Just as a coach is able to assess a player's development, so should Sunday school teachers, youth directors, and even pastors be able to assess a student's spiritual progress. The key is being in a relationship with the student.

Spiritual progression is about far more than passing a test. It is about attitudes, perceptions, visions, hopes, dreams, and questions—things that only people in a relationship can share. When adults invest their lives in teens' lives, they learn more about these areas than any test or assessment can reveal. When adults intentionally help teens understand their spiritual progress, everyone shares a journey of self-discovery.

Within a few moments of listening to a student play a piece of music, a music teacher knows the student's skill level. We expect the teacher to be able to do this, just as we expect the teacher to provide a process by which the student will improve. I propose that the youth ministry team design a format to assess and then assist teens in developing their motivation, their willingness, and their desire to grow.

Some of you may be saying that we cannot assess spiritual formation. I believe that we can. I believe that we can measure a person's knowledge of Scripture. I believe that we can chart progress in an individual's ability to integrate faith into world issues. I believe that we can determine a person's growth in compassion and outreach, and we can determine how his or her effort in the spiritual disciplines affects all these other areas.

Let's admit that our Sunday school programs are typically hit-or-miss ventures. We *hope* they will have an impact. We *hope* that something will get through. We *hope* that lessons change lives. We have all this *hope*, but no way to determine whether our hope is ever realized.

We comfort ourselves by saying things like, "Well, we may never know the impact this is having on that person, so we just have to believe that what we are offering will some day, somewhere, in some way bring about a result." Maybe we see a small minority of students who are developing spiritually and we feel good about it, but we cannot help but wonder why we are not having more impact on more lives. Yes, we must have hope that what we do will make a difference, but our hope will have a greater likelihood of being realized if we are willing and able to put into action a plan that allows us to track spiritual development.

Why is this important? Because teens all learn at different levels. They are *not* all at the same place, they are *not* all developing at the same pace, and they are *not* all alike. Take a look at any typical teen Sunday school class, and you will find the following divisions:

(1) students who want to be there and are ready to learn;
(2) students who do not mind being there, but the topics do not engage them, and they just sort of tolerate the class, occasionally getting into the discussion;
(3) students who would rather be anywhere else but in that class.

In consultations I find that many Sunday school teachers feel discouraged because no matter how much they prepare, there are some students who are always disruptive at worst, or, at best, are totally open with their expressions of boredom. These Sunday school teachers find themselves getting frustrated with the teens because they feel that the disruptive behavior keeps the teens who want to learn from learning. Given the choice, they would jump at the opportunity to release these disruptive, bored teens to some other class.

Can you blame them? Have you ever been in a class where some of the students were into the lesson, but a few were not? Those few can create problems, but it doesn't take a rocket scientist to figure out what is going on. Disruption and frustration will happen whenever we have a system in which we put everyone in the same class, regardless of a person's development.

Simply put, you have some teens who are ready to learn and others who are not—who do not see the value of the lesson in their lives. So my question is, why do we force teens to sit in classes that they are not ready for? It is abusive to everyone involved, and no one has a good experience. Yet because we have one-size-fits-all Sunday school programs, we try to tough out the difficulties and forge ahead with the lessons. Is this what we call intentional spiritual formation? It is sad to say, but if you are in the majority of mainline churches, the answer is yes, this is what we call Sunday morning spiritual formation.

It seems that each church needs to make a decision. Do we *work* Sunday school so that it is part of an intentional process of spiritual formation? Or do we *have* Sunday school because we have always had it, regardless of the results?

Due to family issues, social pressures, and work, some teens will never do anything more than be involved in Sunday morning, so make the most of the opportunity. We need to assess and provide a Sunday morning spiritual-formation program that meets students where they are, rather than trying to force them into some kind of cookie-cutter formula.

Two Formats of Sunday Morning Spiritual Formation

Churches may decide on any number of different formats for developing a process for spiritual formation, but allow me to present two that both have pros and cons. It is my hope that these will get your team thinking about how to upgrade the level of spiritual formation currently being offered in your church.

These formats are not laid out in their entirety but are presented as a way to get your team thinking. It is important for team members to adjust and modify what they learn to meet the needs of your particular church. My first word of caution is that the team needs to continually evaluate any format to ensure that it produces the desired results in the life of the student and becomes beneficial to the overall ministry of the church.

Format 1: An Intensive Format

The first of these formats is designed according to the specific needs and development of the individual. We cannot implement this approach unless we know or have a good idea of where each student currently is on his or her journey. Therefore, it is important to have assessment tools that will assist the team in obtaining a good baseline portrait of each individual's current level of understanding and faith development.

This process will be marked by future assessments at regular intervals to determine how the student continues to develop. Future assessments will, however, be based on the goals and objectives set in consultation with the teacher and/or the youth director.

It is necessary that the leadership team members also be assessed to indicate their own levels of faith formation and establish a baseline on which to build. Taking these tests with the teens leads to a system of integrity so that the teens will know the adults are in this with them. Be sure the teens understand that the assessment is going to help the leadership team know how to best put together a process of spiritual formation that is personalized for them.

The number one priority during the assessment process is to *avoid judgment*. We assess in order to know how to best serve the individual. Possible areas of assessment follow.

Biblical literacy: It is important to discover where our teens are in basic biblical literacy. Something as simple as a basic information test of the Old and New Testaments will help us determine their literacy levels.

Biblical theology: What do the teens believe about God, sin, salvation, redemption, forgiveness, and a whole host of other concepts? An assessment can be something as simple as having the teens write out their faith journeys. Or you may have them write (or talk about) answers to questions like: What does Jesus mean to you? What do you understand about the relationship of Jesus to God? What does salvation mean to you? Describe your understanding of sin and forgiveness. These kinds of questions will help build a baseline to guide the ministry team.

Worship: What do the teens know about the importance and need for community-based worship? How do they feel about the style and effectiveness of the current worship experience? What would they change about the current worship? What do they find most meaningful? What do they think sermons should be about?

Compassion and outreach: What do the teens know about the call to be agents of reconciliation and healing? How do they understand the church's ministry to and with those who are suffering in poverty? How do we live out the compassion of Christ in a world where people have hidden pain? How do we live compassionately at home with our families?

Spiritual disciplines: Do the teens know what these are? How often do they practice these disciplines in their lives? How often do they read their Bibles? When and where are they likely to pray? Do they have friends they talk to about their beliefs and attitudes toward God and spirituality?

Desire to develop spiritually: In this section, we want to measure the teen's desire to develop his or her spiritual life. This assessment can be as simple as asking teens to rate, on a scale of one to ten, their desire to develop their spiritual lives, their prayer lives, their understanding of Scripture, their participation in worship, and their desire to connect with God on a far deeper level. We need to lay the groundwork that spiritual formation is not about learning enough to pass a test, but rather it is about learning how to encounter the awesome presence of God in our hearts and in our daily lives.

Do not worry about where to find these "tests" or how to give them to the teens. This kind of assessment can involve in-depth testing, or it can involve asking a few questions that teens can respond to verbally or in writing. It can be done over a weekend retreat, an overnight, or during a series of Sunday mornings. If you already have adults who are investing their lives in teens, then these adults can casually converse with teens to assess their spiritual development.

The teens' answers will provide keen insight into where they are and how they currently see themselves as disciples of Jesus Christ. Their answers will provide a baseline that will become the beginning point in helping them develop spiritually.

Key for the team to remember is that no matter what the results, everything will help us understand the teens we are serving. When we have no way of assessing them, are we truly providing them with meaningful spiritual formation?

I maintain that we cannot adequately serve our teens until we understand them and know where they are in their journeys. So it is totally OK if we discover that they have little knowledge or understanding. It is OK if we discover that teens who have gone through confirmation really do not have a vital understanding of the church. It is even OK if we personally have taught the same kids for years, only to discover they have never really connected what they learned in church to their everyday lives.

We may be surprised to discover that some of our teens have had profound spiritual experiences and are totally on the journey into the heart of God. But we will never know unless we ask them or become involved in their lives. Not knowing our teens causes us to perpetuate a canned program year in and year out, with the hope that somebody at some time will make a connection between what happens in church and what takes place in the world. Our teens deserve so much more than this hit-or-miss strategy.

If we want to develop our teens as mature disciples of Jesus Christ, then we have to implement strategies that produce results based on our teens' learning styles. This will take a lot of work on the part of the youth staff and volunteer leaders. The staff will need to keep current with developments taking place in each student's life. It is a lot of work, but if you are willing to put in the effort, the results will be unlike anything that you or the entire congregation could have ever imagined.

When the results of the assessments are in, teaching teams can begin to design lesson plans for specific teens. If possible, group the teens with others who are assessed to be at or near the same place on their journeys. This will allow the adults to build on the concept of accountability and to enforce the idea that spiritual formation is always done within community.

It is important for the teens to realize that in taking these assessments, they are not competing with each other. The team is not trying to see who is better, but is attempting to gain a snapshot that will allow the students to better understand who they are and where they are on their faith journeys.

With lesson plans designed around individual faith development, teens will be able to engage the spiritual life in a meaningful, comfortable way. The central thread that binds all these classes will be an emphasis on the spiritual disciplines of Bible study, prayer, worship, and service. No matter what the class level, the spiritual disciplines will tie everything together. At the end of each cycle of lessons, the students will be assessed again in a way that the team determines best. I suggest that the periodic assessments be far less involved than the original baseline assessments.

The periodic assessments will provide the team with important glimpses into the teens' desire for the spiritual life. The team will be able to begin seeing what barriers may be hindering their faith formation, or it may discover someone who is opening to the spiritual life in a way not thought possible.

In this process, progress is based on the student's desire and willingness to take on more in-depth study. The student does not change classes at the end of the year just to move up to his or her corresponding school grade, because this process has little to do with an individual's grade in school. (Remember the karate class, where everyone begins at the same place.)

I believe it is important to keep students with others their age, but it is even more important that a standard of expectation be set so that the students are growing in their understanding of who they are as disciples of Jesus Christ. No, we will not make an eighth-grader sit in a class with first-graders, but this system may offer three or four eighth-graders the same content being taught to first-graders.

As you enter this process, you may discover teens who really do not want to be there. What happens to them? This is a difficult situation, because our cultural tradition has been that if a child is brought to Sunday school, he or she will get religious education. Simply put, we have become accustomed to providing a service, and some people come so that their kids get that service, regardless of the quality.

I know that this is going to be radical to some in Christian education, but I am of the opinion that if students do not want to be involved, we do not force them into something they are not ready to do. How many of us ever truly excel at something that we do not want to be involved in? How many of us get enthused about being part of something for which we have no passion? It does not take long in sports or music to realize who is there because they want to be, and who is there because they have to be.

Yes, there are many examples of people who were forced to attend and turned out to be competent, productive, and effective disciples of Jesus Christ. Do not forget, though, that these are the exceptions. We want teens involved in our process because they want to be, not because they have to be or are forced to be. If some teens truly do not want to give this process a chance, you may offer some alternatives of what they can do during this time on Sunday mornings.

Perhaps they can help get the sanctuary ready, read stories to children, sing in the choir, serve as ushers, or be part of the church hospitality team. This is not bad, and it is not an indication that your system has failed. What it means is that your system is going to do something that has not been done in the last two hundred years: recognize the fact that there are teens who would rather be anywhere else on Sunday morning than at church. If we are willing to acknowledge it, we can work with it. Our goal is to awaken teens to the spiritual life, but we can allow the awakening to take place in a loving environment that lets them to be who they are in this given moment.

What is always going to happen, regardless of whether teens are actively involved or not, is that there are adults who will be connecting with them and entering into mentoring relationships with them. So even if a teen decides he or she does not want to be part of this system and would rather clean the sanctuary, we are going to be sure that the teen is paired with an adult(s) who will begin building a relationship. The purpose of this relationship is to stay connected with the teen and to begin seeking out ways to challenge him or her to enter the deeper life.

Herein lies the ultimate strength of this entire process. Regardless of the curriculum decided on, the most important factor is the adult-teen encounter. Each level of instruction needs to be staffed by people who see the lessons as secondary to the relationships they are developing with the teens in their classes. By intentionally developing these relationships, teachers will be able to have a deeper understanding of—and a greater appreciation for—the students in their classes.

For this reason, the ideal class size for an adult mentor would be four to six students. This relational ministry will move beyond Sunday morning, so be sure you check out other books on relational evangelism. It will be through these relationships that trusting friendships are built as the teens come to realize that the adults truly care about them.

In many churches, this may mean having two or more teen-level classes. The more classes you can have and the more adults you have involved, the greater the possibility for high-level, meaningful results in the lives of your teens. It becomes important that the adult team meet regularly to discuss, share, and pray for each other and for the teens involved in the process.

New Students Enter the Process

Whenever new students arrive or join the church, they are given the baseline assessment and then enter the process. No, you do not just throw them into the test, but rather you talk to them about the goals and objectives of your church's style of Christian formation. (When possible, talk with the entire family.) You let them know what you are all about, and you tell them that the best way to assist them is to know where they are in their journeys. This process is no different from being assessed for any sporting or musical activity.

Last week, my daughter tried out for softball at the YMCA. By watching her bat, catch, and throw, the program directors were able to assess her abilities as a ballplayer. Parents never question this—it is an assessment, not a judgment—and when athletes want to get into a sport, they accept this as a way for coaches to determine which areas are strong and which need to be developed.

Again, if teens decide not to be assessed, the program team graciously accepts that and places them in one of the alternative settings. Always handle these situations with love and compassion in order to show the students that they can enter the program whenever they desire. Right then, the relationship-building begins, and as relationships develop, the teen will connect to the process for spiritual formation.

A Word About Curriculum

I want to stress that curriculum is going to be based on the different levels of classes to be offered. It will be grounded in the church vision and mission statement, and it must be flexible enough to meet the needs of the students, rather than forcing student conformity. I am not going to get detailed about what should be used, because here I am, sitting at a computer, not knowing you or your church.

The reason this cannot be a canned program is because every church is different. Every church has different levels of commitment among the spiritual-formation team. Every church may create a variation of the suggested format to meet the specific needs of its congregation. The most difficult aspect of this intensive approach is that it demands far more involvement from adults than what is typically required to run a traditional Sunday school program. Your team, better than anyone else, will be able to use a variety of materials to design effective spiritual-formation sessions.

You might want to consider keeping the sessions to four- to six-week modules, and then have opportunities at the end of each module for the entire teen group to gather for donuts and fellowship and to thank God for the things learned during the session. You may even want to offer special recognition to students who have completed certain goals, such as Scripture memorization, original written prayers, attendance, essays, keeping a prayer journal, and so forth.

During the year, schedule field trips to nursing homes, prisons, hospitals, and food distribution centers to give the teens an opportunity to live out their faith in acts of compassion and service. Field trips are a good break for teens, and they really will open their hearts and their eyes to what God may have them do as disciples of Jesus Christ.

OK, have I overwhelmed you yet? I can just hear your thoughts about this. You are like, "Dude, this is just waaaay too much work! We can barely get people to cover the classes as it is, let alone have people willing to give time to assess and intentionally watch for faith development."

Now where did I say this would be easy? Do you want a process for spiritual formation that will awaken a deeper sense of the spiritual life, or do you want an easy cookie-cutter program that is proven to be a hit-or-miss venture for the vast majority of teens?

You are right. This is not going to be easy. It is going to be far more involved than what most churches currently do or what most churches are even willing to do, but this method will produce results. It will help teens develop and mature as disciples of Jesus Christ. If you think the first format is too involved, however, let me introduce a second that is a variation on the first.

Format 2: An Alternative Format

This format is not as involved as the first with regard to assessment tools; however, it does involve more adult leaders than are traditionally required. The second format is simply offering a teen elective series on Sunday mornings.

Have the spiritual-formation team meet with the teen youth council (or a group of teen leaders if there is no formal council) to inquire about the kinds of electives they would like to see offered. Once a list has been compiled, teens can choose a class to stay with for a designated amount of time (four to nine weeks), and when the session is over, they can try something different. By offering electives, the spiritual-formation team is providing interest-based programs, and teens will be more inclined to learn if they are able to choose what they study during a given time period.

Now this format is far more involved than just providing interest-based classes. As always, the key component is the student-teacher relationship. The class is about providing an opportunity for teens and adults to connect in order to develop mentoring relationships. It is from these relationships that the program will continue to develop and expand as the adults invest their lives in the teen's lives. It is in this process of interaction that the adults will discover who the teens are and how they understand their faith journeys.

Here are some suggested interest-based, four- to nine-week class possibilities:

Bible Study on a Specific Book in the Bible: Choose a book in the Bible, and begin to uncover its meaning and purpose in the life of a Christian. The teen council may suggest several books in the Bible that are of particular interest to teens. Use the books they select as entry points for Bible study with teens.

Christianity 101: What does it mean to be a Christian today? What are salvation, sin, and redemption? Explore with teens what it means to be a disciple of Jesus Christ in our culture. This course can be a great opportunity to dispel myths and false images.

Understanding Christian Response to Current Issues: This class will use the local newspaper alongside the Bible to discuss how Christians are called to respond to the events that happen around them every day. What were the week's headlines? What might God have to say about certain issues? What is our Christian response to these issues?

This class needs to have a nonjudgmental ground rule. The baseline is that this class seeks to uncover how God is calling us to be in this world, not to judge one another's ideas and beliefs.

Sports/Recreation Activity: If your church has a gym or a field next to it, why not allow some of the teens to play basketball, softball, or another sport during the Sunday school hour? Remember, the key thing here is to allow people to be who they are and where they are. In this system, even if they are playing basketball, they are doing it with adults who are building relationships with them.

In this class, it is important to begin with prayer and end with a short devotional. This is an excellent class for teens who have traditionally shown no interest in sitting through a lesson. They will still be interacting with caring adults who want to get to know them.

Reviewing Movies from a Christian Perspective: Movies have underlying themes and messages. In this class, show movie clips, and discuss their meanings and purposes in light of Scripture, as well as what we are called to be and do as disciples of Jesus Christ. (Be sure that your church obtains the appropriate licensing permissions to use the clips you choose.)

Entering the Mystical World of Prayer: Obviously, this is a class about prayer, but it is far more than talking about different forms of prayer—it is a class to *experience* different forms of prayer. Students will have opportunities to discuss prayer experiences as they are exposed to the vast number of ways prayer can be practiced.

These are just a few of the types of electives your youth ministry can offer. A great deal of assessment information can be gleaned simply from which electives are chosen. Ultimately, we want to guide teens to the electives that will move them more deeply into spirituality, but by offering an array of choices, we begin to see who is ready to make the move and who is still considering making it. As the adults build relationships with the teens, they will begin to get a clearer picture of who the teens are and how to encourage them to take the next step.

There may be some teens who want to take recreation class just because they are not all that interested in the spiritual life. As we said before, this is totally OK! Resist the temptation to think that recreation is just a waste of time. Remember that during the recreation, teens will be building relationships with adult youth ministry team members, and this will never be wasted time.

The idea is to surround these teens with adults who love them and care about them so much that they are willing to take the time to really get to know the teens. They are willing to meet with other members of the spiritual-formation team to discuss and talk about how students are progressing, where there are barriers, and what can be done in order to assist students as they transition to new places in their discipleship journeys.

Sunday Morning—An Entry Point for Teens

We have discussed just two formats of one aspect of spiritual formation in the church. We have not looked at how to utilize youth-group night, midweek studies, accountability groups, service opportunities, retreats, or any other component in an overall strategy for spiritual formation. I have intentionally chosen to deal only with Sunday morning because it is the optimal time we have with teens, and, apart from youth group, it can be the greatest entry point to so much more.

There will be teens who enter the process of spiritual formation through the youth program, especially when they start to get serious about reaching their friends—and it will happen. Yet most teens will enter through the Sunday morning program. Sunday morning is literally our bread-and-butter ministry for spiritual formation and evangelism. We ought to give Sunday morning the best design possible to encourage, enthuse, motivate, inspire, and move people, regardless of age, to deeper levels of faith development. Creativity is *not* the primary motivator for Sunday morning spiritual-formation classes. The primary motivator is designing an intentional spiritual-formation program based on the needs of those involved.

Hey, youth leaders! I emphatically challenge you not to give up this time slot. Be sure to help teens see that Sunday morning is a viable and important component of the overall strategy of youth ministry. If used in conjunction with a spiritually passionate and inspiring worship service, this Sunday morning ministry can be an effective and powerful next step for teens who enter the church through youth ministry.

Your core teen leaders will continually be able to encourage their friends and youth group attendees to come to the Sunday morning program. If the program is truly meeting needs, and if the relationships are developing between adults and youth, then they will be inspired to encourage their friends to be part of this total ministry. Ultimately, the process of intentional spiritual formation will be the foundation from which will arise an overall ministry that has a long-term impact on the teens in the church and the congregation as a whole.

Recruiting Teachers

Everything you have just read is based on the assumption that your church has adults who are intentionally on their spiritual journeys. Here is where I have discovered most educational models break down.

Let's imagine for a moment that we are in a perfect world, where you have a church full of adults seeking to be mature disciples of Jesus Christ. In this perfect world, the adults recognize that they are models for teens. In this perfect world, the adults themselves are actively involved in a process of spiritual formation that continually opens the power of God in their lives. In this perfect world, adults are involved in spiritual-life classes, Bible studies, accountability groups, and prayer teams, and they regularly participate in acts of mercy and social justice. In this perfect world, these adults know how critical it is to provide viable faith-formation opportunities for the youth, and they are beating down the youth pastor's door for the chance to mentor and guide teens. If it could only be possible! This perfect world may exist somewhere, and I think it is called heaven!

I know it sounds like I am beating the proverbial dead horse, but the only way to have any kind of effective teen program of faith formation is to have a viable program of faith formation for adults. As you can see, it really takes a good number of adults to be involved in an intensive ministry of mentoring teens.

Wouldn't it be great if we could get adults to take assessment tests? It would be awesome to see where they are and what they really understand about Christ and the nature and ministry of the church. Our pool of adult mentors will grow only to the extent that our church develops a method of faith formation for adults. No matter which process of faith formation we select, we need to evaluate how we recruit Sunday school instructors and what qualifications we require for them.

What are the typical qualifications in a mainline church? As noted in Chapter Two, it seems that the only real requirement is whether the recruit has a pulse! I am being facetious here, but isn't there some truth to this?

C'mon, be real. Does your church have an intentional recruitment strategy that seeks out those who have demonstrated a knowledge and understanding of what it means to be a disciple of Jesus Christ? How many times have Sunday school teachers been asked to share their faith stories? Do we even know if our Sunday school teachers have faith stories? Is there any requirement for them to have passed some kind of course that qualifies them to be Sunday school teachers? Are teachers expected to be in worship?

I say again, the main qualification seems to be that this person have a pulse. Don't worry. This is not about starting a witch-hunt. The issue is not that we need perfect people to teach class, but that we need people who are intentionally on faith journeys.

We have already talked about how funny church parents can be in dropping off their children on Sunday morning and never even giving a thought to whether the teacher is qualified to guide their children. When did a parent ever ask the teacher to share his or her faith story with them? I will give parents the benefit of the doubt and say that they probably assume that if people are teaching Sunday school classes, then they are somehow qualified to do so. But if we are aware of that assumption, shouldn't we be doing everything we can to ensure its accuracy?

Many Sunday school departments know that the driving force behind their choice of instructors is not the teachers' qualifications, but the need for teachers. The department simply needs someone willing to teach the class, and frequently, the person greeting parents at the door is willing to be that person. Too often, people agree to teach a class because they have a child that age or because no one else will come forward. Sometimes, they teach if they can team up with someone else, so they do not have to be responsible for every Sunday.

Now you are probably thinking that if you had some kind of qualification system, there might well be no one teaching Sunday school. I ask you, is that so bad? Right now, the majority of churches have Sunday school for no other reason than they have always done it. This really inspires, doesn't it? "We need to do this because we have always done it." I just get chills thinking about that kind of motivation.

Seriously, I know that this mainline mantra does hold tremendous power in a church, even if what we have always done makes no sense, yields few positive results, and has little relevance in anyone's life. So the idea of not doing it becomes unthinkable. Yet do we not have a responsibility to provide the next generation with the best tools to help them discover who they are in Jesus Christ? We become faithful to this responsibility only when we empower people to be effective witnesses, teachers, and mentors to teens.

Here are some hints: When recruiting, do not announce it from the pulpit, and do not put a plea for help in the bulletin. Recruitment happens best when it is done on a person-by-person basis, as we are able to see who is demonstrating a willingness to be on a spiritual journey.

When recruiting, look to people in advanced classes like *Disciple Bible Study, Experiencing God, Christian Believer*, and so forth. People who enter these kinds of extended-study classes are showing a desire to go deeper—to be more intentional about their spiritual journeys. They are showing a willingness to be accountable to others for their journeys.

In addition, look for people who are actively pursuing spiritual activities outside the normal Sunday morning schedule. People who attend spiritual-life retreats like A Walk to Emmaus are good candidates because they are demonstrating their desire to go deeper. People who are involved in accountability groups for the purpose of spiritual growth and prayer are prime recruits. Look to the church prayer warriors—those who are always ready to take any and all prayer requests to the Lord. Those who are involved in social witness and outreach to the community and beyond are also people to tap into for teachers, instructors, and coaches.

These types of activities show a person's desire to take seriously his or her own spiritual journey. It is in these activities and classes that we will find people willing to help guide others. Even current teachers may be looking for ways to more intentionally feed their spirits. Begin to offer teachers continuing faith-formation courses, retreats, and other opportunities that challenge them to grow deeper in their faith journeys with Jesus Christ.

Now the problem is that your church may not have many people involved in any of these kinds of spiritual activities. What to do? We really need to work on a few things here.

First, we need to empower the teachers we currently have. This means inviting them to be part of something that will be far more significant than anything that has taken place in the past.

This will be your opportunity to be a mentor and spiritual friend to these adults and walk with them toward a more intentional understanding of who they are in Christ. Ask them to be part of a teacher's spiritual-formation group, where there will be Bible study, accountability checks, and opportunities for a deeper reality of prayer. As your current teachers enter into this active spiritual formation, their teaching will be taken to a new level. They will see that their church cares for their souls by empowering them to minister effectively and inspirationally.

Second, we need to ensure that our church is developing a process for spiritual formation. How are adults being challenged to grow spiritually? How active are the adult Sunday school classes? Have any new classes been added over the past year? Are there classes that go beyond simply discussing a Bible passage to actively helping adults understand who they are as disciples of Jesus Christ? Are adults recruited to participate in programs like *Disciple Bible Study* and Emmaus? Churches that are turning around are doing so because of their renewed emphasis on Bible study and prayer, which leads to a deeper understanding of who we are called to be in this world.

Ensuring that we have a viable process for adult discipleship is more important than getting our teen program off the ground. In all truth, if we had to, we could maintain the current teen program until we developed our pool of adults into spiritual guides, mentors, and friends. In order to increase the spiritual development of our youth, they must be engaged by adults who are actively and passionately on authentic spiritual journeys themselves. Therefore, I want teachers who are:

- involved in Bible study;
- able to articulate their faith stories;
- able to guide, rather than lead;
- able to offer questions, rather than statements;
- willing to pray publicly;
- willing to encourage and assist teens in reaching levels they never thought possible.

Our potential spiritual guides may not have all these characteristics in the beginning. They will not ever be perfect, and every one of them will still have room for growth; however, we need to be able to see in them the willingness to grow, to be stretched, and to become students as well as guides. This potential will provide our faith-formation ministry with the kinds of teachers who will make a difference in teens' lives.

Guess what? These people are in *every* church! They may not know it; they may not have awakened their potential yet, but it is there waiting to hear God's call. And the awakening can only happen when we actively provide opportunities for it to take place.

If your youth ministry is going to be strong and go the distance, it is crucial that there be an intentional approach to discipling teens. There is no way around this principle. All other principles hinge on your church's ability to develop an effective system for making disciples.

Now What?

1. Describe the current process of faith formation for teens in your church.

_____

_____

_____

_____

2. How would teens describe the process of faith formation that they encounter in church?

_____

_____

_____

_____

3. What areas of spiritual formation does your team feel are critical for teens to grow into mature disciples of Jesus Christ?

_____

_____

_____

_____

4. If you were to start tracking the spiritual formation of your teens, what process would you use? How could you develop a process that would not feel like a competition? Put down your ideas below; then meet with your team (and include teens) to get ideas and input.

_____

_____

_____

_____

How would progress in this faith-formation process measured?

_____

_____

_____

_____

How would it be celebrated?

_____

_____

_____

_____

5. What would have to happen before your congregation could move beyond a grade-level model to a model that directly affects teens where they are in their faith formation?

_____

_____

_____

_____

6. What intentional process is there for teacher recruitment in your current system?

_____

_____

_____

_____

_____

_____

_____

How might that change if you initiated a more focused emphasis on faith formation?

_____

_____

_____

_____

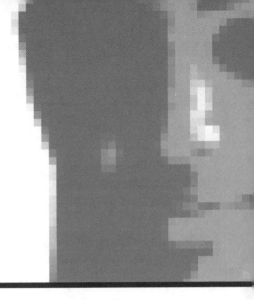

Chapter Seven
Principle #6

A healthy youth ministry is
in constant transformation.

A t first, I had trouble accepting this statement as a foundational principle for effective youth ministry. It is this principle, however, that explains why many of our churches fade away. Both the inability to change and hostility toward change are having a detrimental effect on the mainline church's ability to reach new generations with the Gospel.

I have come to believe that not only is this a foundational principle, but it also needs to be a core value that becomes embedded in the heart and mind of a local congregation. Throughout this chapter, we will move toward a way of building change as a constant to be embraced, rather than a word to fear. So let's charge ahead and face one of the most common statements heard in mainline churches.

"I Hate Change!"

This statement seems to be a constant in many churches today. In fact, I think that when you join a long-established church, they should give you a bumper sticker with this slogan to remind you that the core value of the church is to hate change. I have literally come to believe that the word *change* is actually a dirty word in the mainline church. You say it, you suggest it, or you even think it, and the "I hate change" mongers will be out in full force letting you know why things are the way they are, and why they should stay that way!

Right now you may be nodding your head with a smile crossing your lips, or you may be breaking out in a sweat because I am hitting a nerve. If you have worked in the life of the church for any length of time, you have faced this attitude toward ministry in general, and perhaps toward your ministry in particular.

Well who really does like change? It has been said that the only people who like change are babies. The rest of us like what is comfortable, we like what is expected, and we like what we know. Even if we do not like it, we fight for it because it is what we know. So down with change!

Change Is Essential for Spiritual Transformation

It is funny to me that we struggle so much with a concept that is central to our spiritual journey. The spiritual life calls us to be in a constant state of transformation. Not once in a while, not when we feel like it, but in constant daily transformation—that is *change*. In Paul's letter to the Colossians, he writes:

> Do not lie to each other, since you have taken off your old self with its practices and have **put on the new self, which is being renewed in knowledge in the image of its Creator**. Here there is no Greek or Jew, circumcised or uncircumcised, barbarian, Scythian, slave or free, but Christ is all, and is in all. (Colossians 3:9-10, NIV)

It seems reasonable that we are called to live lives transforming daily into the image of our Creator. Wow! This is some heavy stuff. We are to be renewed in the image of God. Get out of here! This is a call to change from the life we once lived to the life we are called to live in Jesus Christ. This kind of renewal is daily—it is a renewal that will last a lifetime.

I do not know if I have ever met anyone who had actually completed the transformation process. In my Wesleyan tradition, we call this concept of daily transformation and renewal "going on to perfection." We believe that this going on will encompass our whole lives and that reaching perfection is the goal that we work toward. The only way we can even hope to achieve the goal is to work daily at renewing (changing) our hearts and minds into the image of Jesus Christ.

It is a good goal—it helps us with direction and reminds us that we are all on the journey toward perfection in Christ. So if we are called to daily transformation and challenged to grow in our spiritual lives, why do we always seem to struggle so much with change in the church? My only conclusion is that clergy members, myself included, have not been teaching the spiritual life very well.

We clergy have become comfortable with a religion that is more about appeasing people than challenging them to be faithful disciples of Jesus Christ. Now, after all these years of neglecting to teach people about the daily need for renewal, the church is facing a crisis. Either we change and adapt to the culture around us, or we continue to fade away and wonder why no one comes to church anymore. The more culture changes, and the more the church fights change, the more the church will be relegated to the culture's margins. There, the church is destined to become an impotent, voiceless reminder of an ancient way of doing things.

Our calling in this matter is *huge*. To change anything within the church means facing those who fight change. We have a struggle ahead of us to transform churches from social centers to centers of spiritual formation. For those who attempt it, this effort often causes large doses of trauma and conflict.

Every church I have ever consulted with that was adding a new worship service, looking at blended worship, or attempting to get serious about reaching out to the surrounding community was literally a church in conflict. Every single church! Why the conflict? Because to do something different means change, and people resist change.

I learned early on that church people generally do not mind doing whatever it takes to reach people for Jesus Christ, *as long as* it does not cost money or cause them to change the way they have been doing church. Do you know that I have never been to a church that did not want to reach teens? Yet I have been to plenty that did not want to do whatever it took to reach teens, especially if it meant something had to change. I have never been in a church that did not want to be filled with the sounds of babies and children, but I have been in plenty that did not want to do whatever it took to reach families with children if it meant having to change anything.

Obviously, we can't have it both ways. If we recognize that an element of our church is missing (huge chunks of Baby Boomers, Postmoderns, and Millennials, for example), it means we are missing in how we relate to the culture around us. If we want to add that missing part, something in how we do ministry will need to change. Yet changing means we have to look in that mirror and possibly see that our church has drifted away from its primary task. We are not so sure we want to do that. What we see in the mirror may not reflect the idealized image we have of our church.

In order to reach teens and to have a ministry with a long-term impact, the church needs to be in constant transformation. That's right—the church needs to continually reinvent itself in order to speak the word of Christ to each new generation.

The One True Constant

Change, transformation, renewal—it does not mean the core message ever changes or gets watered down, because our core message is our one constant. **The only true constant for the church, in a culture-rich expression of Christianity, is Jesus Christ!**

Jesus Christ is the only constant we can hold on to in the midst of the call to constantly adapt our ministries to reach the prevailing culture. The message of Jesus Christ is eternal; however, the packaging of that message needs to be in constant transformation so that the truth of Jesus Christ can be heard in a continually changing culture. As I said earlier, failing to adapt the message will move the church farther and farther out to the periphery of the culture, in effect causing the church to become an impotent expression of religion.

Going Backward, or Moving Ahead?

Youth ministry is no different. In the beginning of our study, I told you how so many of my consultations begin with people recounting the time when their youth ministry was vital and full and active. They want the youth ministry back to that level of vitality, and their answer is to try to recreate what they had so long ago. Yet the fact that they no longer have that kind of vital youth ministry is an indication that needed changes were not made in the past. The answer is not to go back to the way it was; the answer is to design a new process for building an effective youth ministry. This new process will necessarily mean change.

What reached high school seniors ten years ago may or may not reach them today. Even if you are reaching teens with your current ministry, you need to be looking ahead, reading about teen culture, and watching for changes in communication that happen constantly. When you are looking ahead, the youth ministry takes on the core principle that transformation of our ministry is taking place right alongside the transformations happening in the culture. Until this core value has been embedded in ministry teams, it will feel strange, especially in the face of what is currently working.

I was recently in a church where a layperson was upset with the changes taking place in worship because, in his opinion, everything was going well enough as it was. He saw that people were coming, and a good feeling was growing in the church. "If it ain't broke, don't fix it."

Well, the church system was not "broke" in the sense that things were bad. The church was comfortable with where it was, and in its comfortable place, it had actually failed to realize it had become broken by neglecting its primary task of making disciples. People in this church liked going to their church, they liked the people they sat next to, and they took good care of their building.

The church, however, was not reaching into the changing community outside its doors. It was not intentional about receiving visitors, and it did not have as many children in Sunday school as before, even though the neighborhood was full of children. Members literally felt good about the comfortable state of being that had fallen on their church.

So in this church, a strategic planning team felt as though these areas of outreach and evangelism needed to be addressed, and in doing so, the team disrupted the comfortable feeling that people had about their church. The team laid out a plan that meant changing how church was taking place, and these changes were threatening. The strategic team was literally not prepared for the amount of hostility it received about its renewal plan. Even if this team had been able to do everything right in the way of informing and listening to people (which it, unfortunately, had not), it would still have had to deal with some level of conflict. People simply do not like change or having to leave their comfort zones.

Teens are no different from adults in this regard. On several occasions, I made the mistake of thinking that teens were more flexible than adults in accepting change, but in just about every case, I was proven wrong. Teens are people, and people, regardless of age, struggle with change. At the same time, we know that our culture is in constant transformation.

The congregation that ignores a changing culture does so at its own peril, as does any youth ministry. We are living in an illusion if we think that our current vibrant ministry will still be strong ten years from now if it does not adapt to cultural changes.

Not long ago, I was consulting with a church that wanted to reach teens. The church had a pretty good ministry with a midweek program, but it was not attracting teens to worship. Teens would come to worship once or twice and not return.

I asked the pastor to show me the sanctuary. When I entered, I noticed two problems right away. First, there was a horrible smell in the sanctuary. It did not take long to track the odor to the aging books in the adjacent church library. Second, I noticed that the wallpaper in the sanctuary was old. In fact, the entire sanctuary looked old, like a home that had not been updated in years.

I told the pastor that I doubted that even I would come to more than one or two worship experiences, because the place just had an old feel and smell. Most young adults and teens would not be comfortable here, for no other reason than the old musty smell was just not appealing.

I asked the pastor to list all the places he could think of where teens hang out. He listed the mall, the theater, the local diner, and school. We began to talk about what these places had in common—they were somewhat new, they had good sound systems, they were colorful, and so forth. I told him that walking into this church was like walking into a museum. There was nothing in this sanctuary that would connect teens to any other areas of their lives. It was literally a foreign experience, and it would be difficult for them to feel any level of spiritual comfort when there was physical discomfort. In order to begin the process of reaching out to teens, there would need to be some simple changes to the sanctuary (move the library, change the wallpaper, increase the lighting, and so forth).

A quick word is needed here about teens who grow up in the church. They will endure a great deal more than teens who are unchurched. Teens who grow up in the church are used to the way it is, and they probably do not even think about it (much like the adult members). On the other hand, unchurched teens, and even new adults, will instantly notice old décor and odors ignored by regular attendees. I tell you this because we may have teens in our outdated churches who do not seem to mind, so we wonder why it is such an issue for others. Just remember that we get used to what we endure, but new people know they have choices.

This is just one easy example of the need for churches to be thought-ful about how they present themselves to our culture. Many of our main-line church sanctuaries are in desperate need of remodeling. The look and feel that one gets when entering these churches comes from an era that no longer exists. Literally, teens can feel as though they are walking through a time machine, and it just feels uncomfortable.

I will never forget the time I visited a wonderful elderly gentleman who had lived by himself for forty years. When I walked into his home, it was like walking into a Smithsonian replica of the typical circa 1945 American home. All the furniture, right down to the radio on top of the refrigerator, was from that era. (He was even playing 1940s Big Band.) For a moment, I wondered if I had somehow stepped back in time. It was a strange feeling—something I had never experienced. It was kind of cool and kind of weird at the same time.

I believe that many unchurched people who enter our sanctuaries experience this same kind of bizarre time travel if we are not careful about keeping our facilities updated. Now look, I don't mean to beat this into the ground, but I want to show how difficult it is to see the need for change in our church. We get used to what is comfortable to us. We get used to what we like, and we lose sight of how our comfort level may, in fact, keep us from our primary task of making and maturing disciples of Jesus Christ.

A "Do Whatever It Takes" Attitude

In order to fully reach this culture for Jesus Christ, we need to be constantly evaluating our ministries and their results. In other words, we cannot become satisfied with our system, with our way of doing things, and with our style. Sooner or later, adjustments will need to be made, and the question is, will we make them? Are we are reaching the culture around us? Or are we just reaching other church people? Are people coming to a saving knowledge of Jesus Christ, or are they just becoming good church people? Are people entering into acts of mercy and social justice, or are they just wondering when the next potluck supper will be?

In order to build a church of constant transformation, church leaders need to be able to cultivate a "do whatever it takes" attitude. Whatever it takes to reach people in our community, we are going to do it! Whatever it takes to reach teens, we are going to do it! Whatever it takes to be a welcoming congregation, we are going to do it!

The leadership also needs to realize that this can-do attitude will be a constant challenge. That's right. Conflict will be a constant in the life of the church. Oh, get a grip, and deal with it.

It is an illusion to believe that we can have a church void of conflict. Just read your Bible, and see what Moses, David, Jesus, Paul, Peter, and others had to deal with in regard to conflict. If you do not want conflict, your choices are limited to moving to a mountain hermitage, where you will spend your days by yourself, or moving to a seaside hermitage, where you will spend your days by yourself. In other words, to engage in community is to engage in an arena where conflict takes place. It is our nature, it is in our DNA, and it is part of our struggle to become fully human. So we either learn to work with it, or we let it destroy us to the point where we see that the only alternative is to quit.

The problem is not that we have conflict; the problem is how we deal with conflict. Many church issues could be defused if people would just listen and talk with one another.

Most often, I have discovered that conflict happens in the midst of change because people are fearful that something they have held dear will no longer be the same. It is essential that we listen and work with people in the midst of our can-do attitude. By modeling compassion, care, and love in times of conflict, we model for our teens the power of the Spirit to guide us, even when we may not agree with one another.

What a powerful witness we can give when so many see conflict as the source of divorce and discord! In our disagreement, in our differences, and in our frustration, we can still allow the power of God's love to flow through us, around us, and into us so that we give witness that God is the source of our mission and ministry.

Constant Transformation: A Core Value

If the church as a whole does not understand the core value of the need for constant transformation, it will be difficult to have a vital youth ministry that goes the distance. Remember how everything is interconnected? If our youth ministry defines regular transformation as its core value, but the church does not, then it will be difficult for the youth ministry to remain vital.

Let me state that differently by saying that the youth ministry may remain vital, but it will continually grow more and more disconnected from the overall life of the congregation. It is essential for the youth team and the overall church staff to ensure that ministries work together, adjust together, and progress together. Thus, this principle must be upheld throughout the entire church ministry.

When the entire staff captures the power of this core value, it will have a tremendous impact on all areas of ministry within the congregation. The impact will be especially powerful among our teen leaders, who are our greatest source of knowing how to package the Gospel in such a way that other teens hear and accept it. As we mentor and develop our teen leaders, we will begin to see shifts in the teen culture in each new group that enters the leadership team.

We need to be sensitive to these cultural adjustments so that we can adjust our ministry. Here is the secret to doing this: if we are keyed in to the culture, and if we are sensitive to shifts and adjustments, we can make those shifts and adjustments as we go. This way, the changes do not seem so big.

In many churches, changes seem big because they have not been implemented over the years. So much needs to be done *right now* to bring them up to date that the changes can overwhelm many people.

The teens who learn to value change as part of the church environment are helping the church ministry right now, not just in the future. They are also learning the value of being on top of a ministry in progress. They will be part of the overall process of evaluating whether different ministries are succeeding in reaching their target audiences. These teens will also become a tremendous asset to the adults who are willing to listen to what they say about the strength of their ministry and its ability—or inability—to reach their unchurched friends.

Constant Assessment Leads to Success

In order for our ministry to be successful, we need regular intervals during which the leadership teams listen to feedback from different segments of the church. This feedback becomes a type of assessment test for the various church ministries. If a ministry is found lacking, strategies must be developed to discover what can be done to strengthen it. Some ministries may even need to be dissolved if they no longer produce viable returns.

As you know, I have heard story after story about the initial success of a program or ministry, only to hear about its eventual downfall. People who tell these stories usually point to an individual or a lack of continued enthusiasm when in fact, the program has most likely run its course. Yet in the church it is difficult to let go of anything that meant something to us in the past.

This kind of assessment and listening process can seem highly vulnerable to a leadership team that seeks to build a strong ministry. It becomes important for the teams to recognize that not everything will work, that not everything is going to have a constant success rate, and that not everything will produce measurable results. The team listens to feedback and then makes adjustments in its members' respective leadership areas.

It is crucial that teens be part of this process. Teens must constantly be challenged to evaluate their ministry to see how it can be further developed.

When I first began my ministry as an associate director of youth ministry in the East Ohio Conference of The United Methodist Church, I did not involve teens in the evaluation process, and I made changes without obtaining their input. The results were predictable: the teen leadership council strongly resisted the changes. I have to confess that I considered their resistance a personal attack. Because I felt this way, I became defensive and took a rigid stance.

At the time, I failed to see that the teens' resistance was not personal, and it was not because they did not like the direction I was taking. Their resistance was due to the fact that I did not include them; I did not listen to them or value their input before making a decision to change course. They would have been more receptive had we been able to talk and share the pros and the cons of the proposed changes. Had I taken the time to listen, to share, to dream with, and to open myself to those teens, we all could have saved ourselves some of the pain we went through. We could have ended up with a shared vision and a shared dream. It is a lesson I will never forget.

Over the years, I have found that teens know best what is working—and what is not—in assisting them to grow spiritually and to reach their friends. This really is the difference between a youth ministry *for* teens and a ministry *with* teens. Their input and support provide the necessary changes that lead us to be more effective in our ministry to the congregation in general, and to and with teens in particular.

Success As a Motivator

Success is a motivator for constant transformation. In East Ohio, we have a yearly spiritual-life weekend event that has boomed in attendance. Since 1996, this event has grown from three hundred and fifty participants to over five thousand. You just cannot have that kind of growth and remain the same.

This massive, explosive growth forces our Conference Youth Council to continually adapt in order to keep up. Every year is different from the year before. Our teen council has been awesome at being able to recognize the changes needed to keep up with the growth and give people a great event every year.

Remember, fear of change is not age-specific. All people, regardless of age, resist change. This is going to be difficult for Baby Boomers, many of whom have worked hard to change their churches to allow more contemporary forms of worship. Boomers have now become comfortable with certain styles of music and ways of doing worship. The critical test for Baby Boomers will be their ability to adjust and *change* in order to reach their children and grandchildren.

This is the cultural transition the church finds itself trapped in today. Boomers are finally getting the church to meet their needs, only to be challenged by whether they will be able to continue the transformation for their children and grandchildren. We will see whether they are up to the challenge. We can only hope.

Churches and ministries that continue to grow over a long period of time are those that are constantly in a state of transformation. The key thing for all areas of ministry is not to get comfortable. Keep challenging yourselves, your abilities, and your level of production, and continue to walk lovingly with one another to keep the ministry fresh, vital, exciting, and passionate.

Now What?

Because every church is different, it is difficult to know what changes need to be made in your particular church. Your church may be one of the many that has not changed in the past fifty years. Your church may be functionally able to do ministry in a 1950s culture, but it may be unable to grasp what it means to be a twenty-first-century church.

Friend, if this is the case, there is a lot of change that needs to take place. So let me suggest that you hire a consultant to help your church determine its strengths and growth areas. The consultant will be able to provide insight, suggestions, and, most importantly, an action plan that you can begin to enact in your congregation to move it toward being focused on its primary task in the current cultural environment.

Before implementing any changes, be sure that there are opportunities for people to read and review the action plan. Hold discussions, and encourage people to share how they feel about the changes. It is important that church members realize that the strategy team is taking their concerns seriously, that the team is more willing to listen than to defend, and that the team really cares how people make the transition to a vital twenty-first-century ministry.

The same process can be used for your youth ministry *if* the congregation is already working to be current. Involve the teens to continually evaluate and review their ministry. Talk to them about what is working and what is not. Let the teens know that you are genuinely interested in what they have to say. Let them know that they are valued for their input and for doing what needs to be done to take the ministry to the next level.

As you disciple teens through their personal transformation in being renewed in the image of Christ, they will be open and willing to develop a ministry whose primary mission is to guide teens into vital relationships with Jesus Christ. When this becomes the primary mission, you will literally have to watch out—the teens will get serious, and they will do whatever it takes to reach their friends for Jesus Christ.

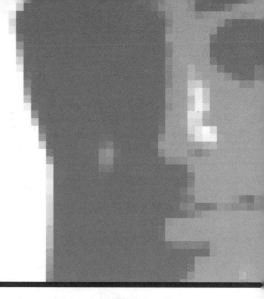

Chapter Eight
Pulling It Together

We have covered six basic principles of building a high-impact, long-term youth ministry for your congregation. Let's review what we have learned.

Principle #1: A healthy youth ministry flows from an intentional ministry of faith formation to and with adults.

Your youth ministry will ultimately be as strong as your intentional ministry to and with adults. When adults are growing spiritually and are willing to go deep, you will have the substance from which a vital, effective, and long-term youth ministry can emerge.

Principle #2: A healthy youth ministry understands the positive expression of teen empowerment.

Teen empowerment is not about who gets to make decisions, who gets to vote, and whose ideas are accepted. Teen empowerment is first and foremost about spiritual empowerment. Teens who are growing spiritually will be effective church leaders now and in the future. Truly empowered teens are the result of being mentored by spiritually empowered adults.

Principle #3: A healthy youth ministry understands the difference between youth activity and youth ministry.

Activity for the sake of activity makes youth group no different from any other teen organization. Activity in youth ministry should always be part of a greater strategy to connect growing, maturing adult disciples of Jesus Christ with teens. Activities facilitate the opportunity for teens to connect with other teens, but more importantly, for teens to connect with adults.

Principle #4: A healthy youth ministry intentionally recruits a diverse team of spiritually open and spiritually developing adult leaders.

The teens you reach out to are wonderfully diverse in the way they understand life, spirituality, politics, school, music, and so forth. We need adults who are diverse enough to enter teens' world. It is okay if our adult team has some different theological understandings, as long as the team is committed to the primary task of helping teens connect with Christ and assisting them in moving deeper into the heart of Jesus.

Principle #5: A healthy youth ministry has an intentional process for teen spiritual formation.

It is not enough for our teens just to be part of our program. There is an agenda, a hope, and a process we want teens to participate in so that they can develop spiritually. The youth ministry's desire is that all teens develop as vital disciples of Jesus Christ. In order for this to happen, there must be an intentional process by which teens are able to develop and grow according to their own individual abilities.

Principle #6: A healthy youth ministry is in constant transformation.

Simply put, the team needs to continually feel the pulse of the ministry in order to adjust and change as needed to keep the ministry fresh, relevant, and able to reach new people for Jesus Christ.

As you can see, there is no quick fix for the youth ministry issues facing churches today. These are hard and true principles that, if followed, will create a youth ministry that goes the distance—that will be with the church over the long run and that will be a high-impact ministry to and with youth.

You can try to circumvent these principles, but the results will always be the same. The youth ministry will stop and start over and over again.

It will be difficult to establish these principles; however, if the church is willing to invest in an effective youth ministry, it must work toward making these principles building blocks within the church.

Throughout this book, I have refrained from telling you exactly what you need to do, from putting together strategies and ideas, and from laying out methods for you to implement. I have intentionally done this because part of the journey is discovering the strategies and methods that work best in your setting.

I cannot tell you what will work for you. I cannot tell you what will work in your congregation, but I can tell you that if these principles are in place, your success rate for achieving your goal of an effective youth ministry will be greatly increased.

Be careful when reading about what worked in someone else's church, because it may or may not work in yours. Your congregation has certain dynamics that are unique to your setting. These dynamics may or may not contribute to the overall ability to replicate what worked somewhere else.

Your church is unique—God has a unique plan for your church and for the ministry to and with all people who are and will be connected to it. The critical factor is to seek God's plan for your church. Discover how God is calling your church to be a unique witness to the love and life power of Jesus Christ in your community.

It is important to be patient with your church. These principles will not be established overnight, nor will they be easy to establish. You are not looking for a quick fix. (If you are, get off it, because it won't last.)

Gather a small team of adults and teens to share this adventure with you. Seek God in prayer, work to create a shared plan, set goals and objectives, and begin your journey with an attitude of compassion and forgiveness.

God is not finished with you or your congregation. You have a calling and a mission to reach out to the world in the name of Christ. Now get going, work the principles, discover God's plan, and believe that you have a purpose to fulfill. God be with you on this incredible journey!

Now What?

Start working the principles.

- Seek out a team of adults and teens, and share with them the principles in this book.

- Talk to your pastor about these principles, and ask him or her to share this vision for the church.
- Explore the possibility of employing a church consultant to assist your church in discovering its strengths and growth areas.
- Evaluate the process for faith formation currently implemented.
- Organize a discussion with church teens to learn what is reaching them, and what is not.
- See about organizing a discussion with teens from the local high school to learn about their impressions of and attitudes toward church and spirituality.
- Begin one faith-formation study for adults and another for teens. Let the process toward a totally revitalized church begin!